Prepare for Discussion

Ted Power

2024

TABLE OF CONTENTS

INTRODUCTION

Prepare for Discussion is for learners of English at the upper-intermediate level or above who wish to improve their participation and performance in discussion, extending their vocabulary to cover a wide range of topics. For each of 28 popular topics there is:

- a vocabulary exercise to define terms

- a short written text

- a dialogue for reading aloud in pairs

- a set of discussion questions

- a themed crossword

There is also a selection of **extracts from the dialogues** which allows functional analysis and systematic practice of the colloquial formulae used in discussion.

The exercise types and activities in *Prepare for Discussion* lend themselves to oral work in groups or pairs and are therefore suitable both for class teaching and one-to-one tuition.

The material is especially relevant to learners preparing to study in academic institutions (e.g. universities in English-speaking countries) where they would be expected to recognise a wide range of vocabulary and to join in discussions.

Use of the materials

Prepare for Discussion sets out to maximise participation and to minimise the disappointment which can occur when students are expected to discuss semi-specialist topics without adequate preparation.

Providing learners with the right vocabulary for a given topic - *"les mots justes"* - is a more successful approach than throwing them into a discussion topic cold i.e. without the resources to deal with it. Once teachers see learners reaching for bilingual dictionaries or translation apps on their phones, fluent discourse on particular themes becomes a lost cause. My approach starts by presenting "the right words": the key vocabulary I would expect native speakers to use to handle a given topic. I base this step-by-step approach on the belief that a fundamental part of teaching is to offer learners some guidance and therefore a fair challenge.

The following sequence of work for each topic is recommended:

0.1 **Vocabulary exercises**

The vocabulary exercises should be used for oral work i.e. discussion in pairs or small groups. Given a choice of three different words or phrases, the task for learners is to use contrast and comparison (attribute analysis) to find the "Odd One Out". Words can be related according to different aspects of meaning, so in some cases there will be more than one possible answer. The teacher then brings the class together and the answers are discussed. Note that there are not necessarily any wrong or right answers. It is up to the learner to give reasons for choosing the "Odd One Out", though some reasons are more likely than others.

Learners' receptive vocabulary will be a lot larger than their productive vocabulary. "Odd One Out" exercises are good starting-points for activating vocabulary since they present a limited frame of reference and immediately challenge everybody to participate. By using each set of exercises to focus on a single theme, interest can be developed in topics which learners may otherwise dismiss as not their favourite candidates for discussion.

The topics also have a **Dictionary reference** section found following the discussion questions. Here, some of the terms used as core vocabulary for each topic are defined. The definitions given are in the context of the discussion material and are chosen to facilitate the tasks. For example, learners who are finding the "odd one out" exercise difficult may refer to this section rather than using their own dictionaries. At the discussion question stage, these definitions are also designed to be useful.

0.2 **Short Texts**

These contain the important lexical items contributing to each theme and may be used for listening or reading comprehension.

The comprehension questions appear on pages 169 to 177 and are numbered according to the paragraphs (¶1, ¶2, etc.) in the short texts where the answers can be found. They may be read by either the teacher or by learners working in pairs - one student posing the questions while his/her partner answers, swopping roles halfway through.

Dictation of all or part of a text remains a useful way of testing listening comprehension as well as spelling and punctuation. Learners may recognise words when they see them in a text, but may find difficulty recognising them when they hear them only. Many vocabulary books cover topics comprehensively in writing, but offer little or no chance for students to hear the words being spoken. Students who fail to recognise or to produce the vocabulary orally will only offer a limited contribution to the discussion class, they will fail to increase their range and will not feel they have learnt anything new.

Giving the dictation means that the teacher is the first person to read the short text aloud. Careful attention should be paid to word and sentence stress, since a useful task (see C. Pronunciation below) is mark up of the stressed syllables.

A. Full Dictation

A class of advanced students can do the full dictation straight away. Weaker students can complete the selective dictation instead.

B. Selective Dictation

The teacher dictates the sentence, but asks the students to write down the words in bold print only as a numbered list. Example: Conventional beliefs are the ones which most people share, but alternative beliefs are usually held by minorities. Please write [1] Conventional beliefs [2] alternative beliefs.

C. Pronunciation

The teacher reads the first paragraph of the text aloud and demonstrates how to mark in the word and sentence stress. As the teacher reads further paragraphs of the text aloud slowly, the students continue marking in word and sentence stress using a pencil so that corrections can be made. Note that weak forms, usually short grammatical words, remain unmarked. By working in pairs, students can check their work together. As a final check, the teacher asks individual students to read paragraphs of the text aloud at normal speed using the appropriate stress and intonation patterns.

To mark the stress, place stress marks BEFORE each stressed syllables. The small grammatical words tend to be weak forms, so leave them unmarked. Example:

Con'ventional be'liefs are the ones which 'most 'people 'share, but al'ternative be'liefs are 'usually 'held by mi'norities.

A'mong the 'most 'common al'ternative be'liefs are 'those in'volving 'mediums and

clair'voyants. 'Mediums 'claim to have 'psychic 'powers and 'extra 'sensory per'ception.

0.3 <u>Discussion Dialogues</u>

These are intended for pair work and contain arguments between speakers with opposing views. They have been written to incorporate the discussion techniques analysed in the appendix. Discussion is more than just knowledge of vocabulary. It includes logical argument, agreement and disagreement, questioning, responding and holding the floor.

Learners from certain cultures and educational backgrounds may never have rehearsed the language of argument in a lesson before. They will have little idea of the target until they have been presented with model dialogues containing suitable formulae. It is unfair to expect them to participate in a discussion class without some rehearsal.

A <u>Listening for stress and intonation</u>. These features bring out the meaning.

The teacher reads lines of the dialogue aloud slowly. Students repeat paying careful attention to sentence and syllable stress. They then use a pencil to mark the stresses as in the previous section. Leave weak forms unmarked.

B. <u>Reading aloud</u> (pair work) paying careful attention to stress and intonation.

0.4 <u>Discussion Questions</u>

These are designed to ensure wide coverage of each topic. They are to be used flexibly since students may have better questions of their own.

It is recommended that some or all of the other components of *Prepare for Discussion* should be used before the students are required to hold the discussion. Explain that the groundwork is important to ensure that everybody in the class can participate.

There is no need to attempt all the questions. It is better if students select the questions which interest them most (they should aim to cover at least three questions). There is no need to choose consecutive questions unless they complement one another.

The teacher should decide whether the discussion should be conducted in pairs or small groups (ideally four students of different nationalities including both men & women).

Pair work may be inadvisable if the class includes very weak students who are unforthcoming. However, some students may feel more confident speaking to one other person. A mixture of pairs and groups is another option.

Tell students how much time they have. It is best to require pairs and/or groups to report back. Different tasks can be assigned to group members e.g. chairing the discussion, interviewing, taking minutes, reporting back on different questions.

Do not require individuals to report back on every single word that has been said. It is better to ask different people to report back on what interested them most or what they feel the other members of the class would like to hear about.

0.5   Themed Crosswords

These incorporate the core vocabulary for each topic and can be used either at the end of the scheme of work to consolidate vocabulary or set as homework before the discussion takes place to whet the appetite for exchanging views.

APPENDIX :   Extracts from the dialogues

(functional analysis of discussion techniques)

The extracts contain colloquial formulae commonly used in discussion. The formulae have been sorted into ten sections, most of which have sub-sections. The main sections are:

1.   Asking someone for their opinion about a topic
2.   Delaying strategies
3.   Presenting a number of arguments
4.   Giving your opinion about a topic
5.   Agreeing
6.   Disagreeing
7.   Countering
8.   Logical argument
9.   Clarification
10. Expressing solutions and alternatives

Instructions for use accompany each section. The extracts may be read by a teacher or by a student's pair work partner. The tasks for the listener are to note and use the colloquial formulae in each of the ten categories as well as to identify the topic from which the extract is drawn.

The list of the 28 discussion topics appears at the beginning of the appendix on page 179.

1. ALTERNATIVE BELIEFS

1.1 Find the "odd one out".

[There may be more than one answer. Give your reasons.]

1. A) astrology B) astronomy C) fortune telling

2. A) a star sign B) a horoscope C) a planet

3. A) to foresee B) to predict C) to convey

4. A) extrasensory perception B) telepathy C) psychic power

5. A) a personality B) an appearance C) a character

6. A) phenomena B) happenings C) seances

7. A) a premonition B) a prediction C) a dream

1.2 Short text (see page 169 for comprehension questions)

Conventional beliefs are the ones which most people share, but **alternative beliefs** are usually held by minorities.

Among the most common alternative beliefs are those involving **mediums** and **clairvoyants.**

Mediums claim to have **psychic powers** and **extrasensory perception**. They invite people to special meetings called **seances** where they demonstrate their ability to talk to the dead and convey their messages to the living.

Clairvoyants claim to **foresee** events and have been known to offer their services both to famous politicians and members of royal families. There are many biblical examples of **fortune telling** including **premonitions** such as Joseph's dream. **Cynics** maintain that accurate **predictions** result from the **laws of probability** and do not provide proof of special powers.

1.3 Dialogue - read aloud in pairs

A: *Do you believe in* horoscopes?

B: *I certainly don't believe in* the ones you see in the popular press *...you know what I mean ...* they give you half a horoscope and a telephone number. If you want the interesting half you are charged 98 pence per minute!

1. ALTERNATIVE BELIEFS

A: *They could still be true.* Everybody has to earn a living!

B: *Yes, but* a serious astrologer would want to know a person's exact date of birth, not just their star sign.

A: *Well, even so, why should* the exact positions of the Sun, Moon and other planets on your date of birth have any connection whatsoever with your personality and the future course of your life.

B: *I suppose it's all part of* your total environment. Scientists don't understand everything, but they often observe links between certain phenomena.

A: *In that case,* would you describe astrology as a science?

B: *It depends* who's doing it.

A: *You could say that about a lot of things* we call sciences.

1.4   Questions - discuss in pairs or groups

1. Do you think there is intelligent life on other planets?

2. Some people claim that they have seen UFOs (Unidentified Flying Objects) such as flying saucers. Do you believe them?

3. What is your opinion of people who say that they can communicate with spirits? Have you ever taken part in a seance?

4. Do you know anybody with psychic powers or extrasensory perception?

5. Do you believe in telepathy? Is there another person in the world with whom you have a special understanding?

6. Would you ever visit an astrologer for a forecast of how your life will run in the future?

7. What does your star sign tell you about your personality and your compatibility with other people?

8. Do you believe in other forms of fortune telling such as (a) palmistry (b) tarot cards or (c) reading teacups?

9. Among the popular superstitions in the UK are Friday the 13th, breaking a mirror, walking under ladders, black cats, knocking on wood, spilling salt, horseshoes, and seeing one or two

magpies. Do you know the significance of each? Can you describe any other superstitions which are commonly held in your country relating to bad or good luck, long life, protection and the avoidance of harm?

Dictionary reference

Astrology: the study of the positions of the sun, moon, planets and stars in the belief that they affect human character and events.

Astronomy: the study of everything in the universe beyond Earth's atmosphere.

Fortune telling: the spiritual practice of making predictions about another person's life through palmistry, crystal ball gazing, reading tea leaves, and other methods.

Star sign: one of twelve specific divisions of the zodiac: Airies, Taurus, Cancer, Leo etc.

Horoscope: a description of what is going to happen to you, based on the position of the stars and the planets at the time of your birth.

Planet: any of the large bodies that revolve around the sun in the solar system.

Foresee: see beforehand or know in advance.

Predict: say what you think will happen in the future.

Convey: express a thought or a feeling so that it is understood by other people.

Extrasensory perception: the ability to know things without using hearing, seeing, touch, taste or smell.

Telepathy: the direct communication of thoughts and feelings between people's minds without the need to use speech, writing or any other normal signals.

Psychic power: the possession of strange mental abilities such as to communicate with spirits, to read the minds of other people or to see into the future.

Personality: the special combination of qualities in a person which makes them different from others in the way that they think, feel and behave.

Appearance: the way someone or something looks.

Character: the way someone thinks, feels or behaves; the mental or moral qualities distinctive to an individual.

1. ALTERNATIVE BELIEFS

Phenomena: observable facts or events.

Happenings: events or occurrences

Seance: a meeting where people try to talk to spirits or dead people.

Premonition: a feeling that something is going to happen.

1.5   Crossword

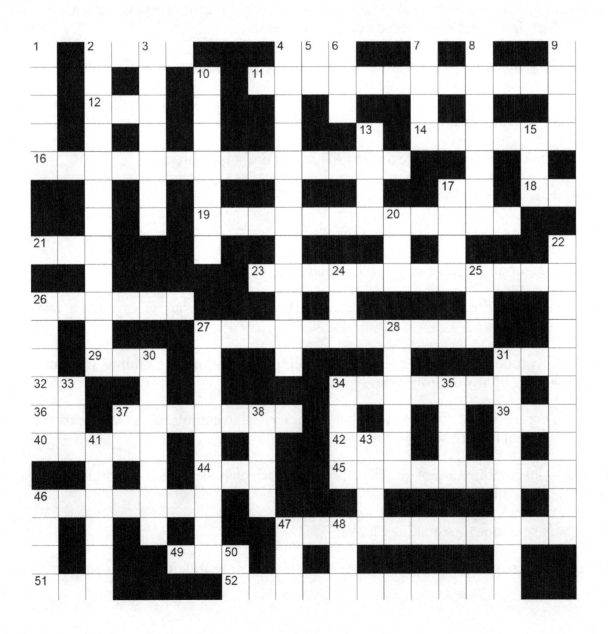

1. ALTERNATIVE BELIEFS

Clues

ACROSS

2. The opposite of go (4)
4. Apple _ _ _ and custard (3)
11. Mainstream (12)
12. Romeo _ _ _ Juliet (3)
14. Not often (6)
16. Saying what your luck will be in the future (7,7)
17. To _ _ or not to _ _ (2)
18. First Person Plural Subject Pronoun (2)
19. Perception of events without using the usual senses (12)
21. After night comes _ _ _ (3)
23. Uneasy feelings about coming dangers (12)
26. To carry or transfer (6)
27. Your character (11)
29. To drink a small amount from a glass (3)
31. In the past (3)
32. Not out! (2)
34. Solid bodies orbiting stars (7)
36. Country or Company (2)
37. Meetings where groups try to communicate with spirits (7)
39. As well (3)
40. The past of stand (5)
42. Third Person Singular Subject Pronoun Female (3)
44. A married woman (3)
45. A reading of your star sign (9)
46. On a _ _ _ _ _ _ _ made for two! (7)
47. Attempts to tell the future (11)
49. Fruit boiled with sugar (3)
51. Much or Many is a _ _ _ (3)
52. Chance (11)

DOWN

1. Evidence (5)
2. People with special powers to see into the future (12)
3. People who receive spirit messages (7)
4. Tabloid newspapers (7,5)
5. The opposite of out (2)
6. New Year's _ _ _ (3)
7. A beautiful shape in the sky (4)
8. Someone who is always anxious (7)
9. Kill (4)
10. Predict (7)
13. Part of the leg which you can bend (4)
15. Not high (3)
17. Three men in a _ _ _ _ (4)
20. Short for Grandma (3)
22. They tell you your horoscope (11)
24. Boys grow into them (3)
25. The holly and the _ _ _ (3)
26. Sceptics (6)
27. Happenings (9)
28. Thinner (6)
30. Tell in advance (7)
31. The study of the stars to tell your future (9)
33. A negative word (3)
34. The opposite of pull (4)
35. Don't put them all in one basket (4)
37. I'm _ _ sorry! (2)
38. The sun rises in the _ _ _ _ (4)
41. Supernatural (6)
43. Little Red Riding _ _ _ _ (4)
46. _ _ _ _ , book and candle. (4)
47. Short for professional (3)
48. Period in history (3)
50. Member of Parliament (2)

1. ALTERNATIVE BELIEFS

Crossword answer key

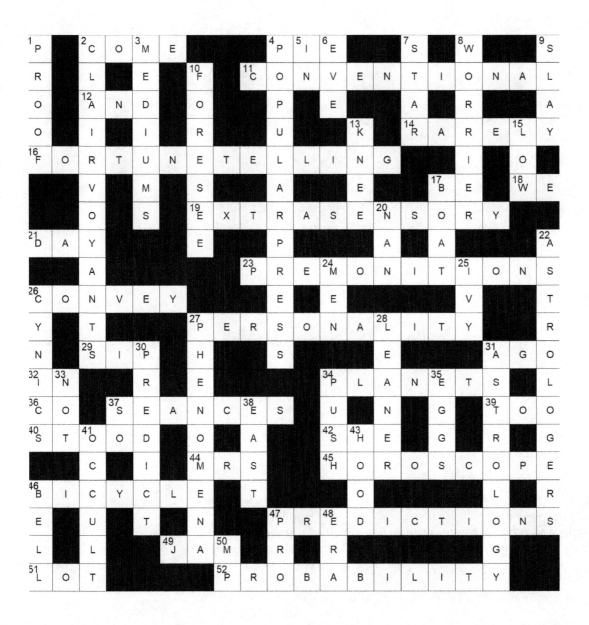

2. ANIMAL WELFARE

2.1 Find the "odd one out".

[There may be more than one answer. Give your reasons.]

1.	A)	cockfighting	B)	dogfighting	C)	bullfighting
2.	A)	a chase	B)	a hunt	C)	a race
3.	A)	civil rights	B)	human rights	C)	animal rights
4.	A)	country life	B)	the urban environment	C)	the countryside
5.	A)	to damage	B)	to hurt	C)	to injure
6.	A)	fatigue	B)	tiredness	C)	exhaustion
7.	A)	tranquillisers	B)	antibiotics	C)	growth hormones
8.	A)	to shoot	B)	to slaughter	C)	to kill

2.2 Short text (see page 169 for comprehension questions)

The British are said to be fond of animals. For many of them a dog or a cat is part of the family and must be well looked after.

Large sums of money are spent on **veterinary bills** and **pet food**. A trip to a supermarket will reveal whole aisles dedicated to our animal friends.

However, in the same supermarket, you can find **battery chickens** which have been **factory farmed** in cramped conditions and injected with **antibiotics** to contain disease, **growth hormones** to fatten them for market and **tranquillisers** to stop them from going mad.

Aware of the contradictions in their treatment of animals and the risks of **mad cow disease**, many British people are turning to **vegetarian diets**. Some have joined **animal rights groups** and have taken part in protests against **the meat trade**, especially the export of live animals for **slaughter** overseas.

2.3 Dialogue - read aloud in pairs

A: *What do you think of* fox hunting?

7

2. ANIMAL WELFARE

B: *I'm completely against it.*

A: *But if* you worked on a farm and your chickens were killed by foxes, *you'd think differently.*

B: *I doubt it.* People who keep all those hounds and dress up in colourful costumes really enjoy killing foxes. *Besides,* it's such a cruel way to kill them.

A: *Do you really think so?* Once the first dog has caught up with the fox, death is fairly instant.

B: *You seem to forget that* the fox is already dying of exhaustion after a long chase. Then it's torn to pieces. *If* farmers really need to kill foxes, *why don't they just* shoot them? There'd be far less damage to the countryside without hunts.

A: *But* fox hunting is part of country life. It's one of our traditions.

B: *That's beside the point.* Dogfighting and cockfighting were traditions and so was slavery before we became a more civilised society by making these things illegal.

2.4 Questions - discuss in pairs or groups

1.   Many vegetarians believe that factory farming is a cruel and unnecessary practice and that our diets would be healthier if we ate less meat. Do you agree?

2.   Animal rights protesters argue that the export of live animals for slaughter is uncivilised and should be prohibited under international law. Do you agree?

3.   "Keeping animals in zoos, circuses or dolphinariums to entertain human beings is selfish and inhumane." Do you agree?

4.   Bullfighting, fox hunting and whaling are part of some countries' traditions. Do you think that Spain, England and Japan have a right to continue these traditions?

5.   "The British spend far too much money on household pets. They would do better to have fewer cats and dogs and to use the money to help poor and hungry people." What do you think?

6.   Would you ever wear a fur coat?

7.   Is it right to use animals for medical research or to test cosmetics?

Dictionary reference

Chase : the act of hurrying after someone or something in order to catch him, her or it.

2. ANIMAL WELFARE

Hunt: the act of pursuing (a wild animal) for sport or food.

Race: a contest of speed as in running, swimming, driving or riding etc..

Civil rights: guarantees of equal social opportunities and equal protection under the law regardless of race, religion or other personal characteristics.

Human rights: the basic freedoms which belong to every person in the world.

Animal rights: the rights of animals to live free from human exploitation and abuse.

Country life: the lifestyle associated with those who live in rural areas, as opposed to living in cities or their suburbs.

The countryside: the land and scenery of a rural area.

Damage: do physical harm that impairs the value, usefulness or normal function of something.

Hurt: cause physical or emotional pain to someone.

Injure: do physical harm to someone.

Fatigue: extreme tiredness resulting from mental or physical exertion or illness.

Tiredness: the feeling that you are in need of rest or sleep.

Exhaustion: a state of extreme physical or mental tiredness.

Tranquillisers: medicinal drugs taken to reduce tension or anxiety.

Antibiotics: medicines that fight bacterial infection by destroying microorganisms.

Growth hormones: present in humans produced by the brain's pituitary gland to govern height, bone length and muscle growth or anabolic agents injected in animal production to help them grow faster

Shoot: kill or wound a person or animal with a bullet or arrow.

Slaughter: kill (often used when killing animals for food)

2. ANIMAL WELFARE

2.5 Crossword

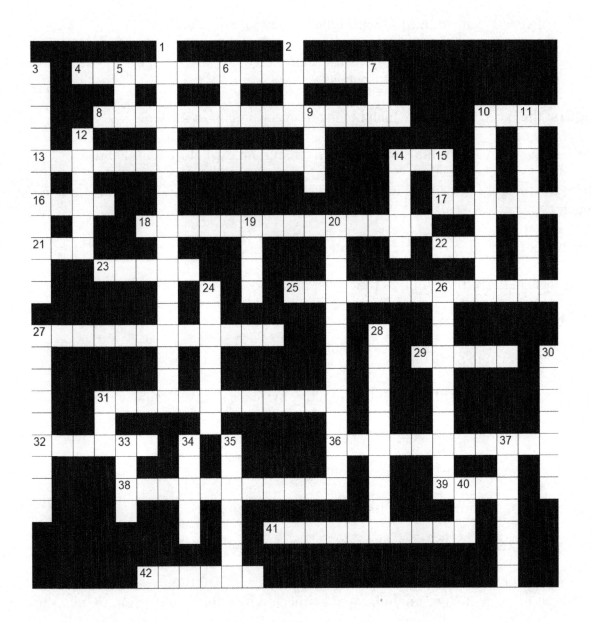

2. ANIMAL WELFARE

Clues

ACROSS
4. Birds which are fed under artificial light (7,8)
8. Menus for people who refuse to eat meat (10,5)
10. _ _ _ _ or any (4)
13. Pills to calm people or animals down (14)
14. Container for rubbish (3)
16. 12 months (4)
17. Fair treatment of humans or animals (6)
18. Substances injected to increase body size (6,8)
21. Skating on _ _ _ (3)
22. The abbreviated name for "animal doctor" (3)
23. The pursuit of an animal, for example (5)
25. Produced through intensive agriculture (7,6)
27. A contest between two farmyard birds (12)
29. Fire a gun (5)
31 Ripped into small bits (4,2,6)
32. Revenue (6)
36. Substances stopping the growth of bacteria (11)
38. Living in rural surroundings (7,4)
39. Aim or target (4)
41. Physical and / or mental fatigue (10)
42. Dogs for hunting foxes (6)

DOWN
1. Animal doctor (10,7)
2. A small picture or symbol or a much admired person (4)
3. Rural surroundings (11)
5. The definite article (3)
6. Automobile (3)
7. Please _ _ _ down (3)
9. Hurry (4)
10. Kill (9
11. Industry which prepares and sells animals for consumption (4,5)
12. Harm to people or property (6)
14. The Alsatian is a popular _ _ _ _ _ of dog (5)
15. Neither... _ _ _ (3)
19. Injury or damage (4)
20. An illness affecting bovine animals (3,3,7)
24. Nourishment for dogs and cats (3,4)
26. Pursuing a doglike mammal for sport (3,7)
27. Not barbarous or primitive (9)
28. Old customs or practices (10)
30. Put on a costume or special clothes (5,2)
31. Also (3)
33. Make fun of (4)
34. Organised chases to kill animals (5)
35. Chased or followed (7)
37. Against the law (7)
40. Possess (3)

2. ANIMAL WELFARE

Crossword answer key

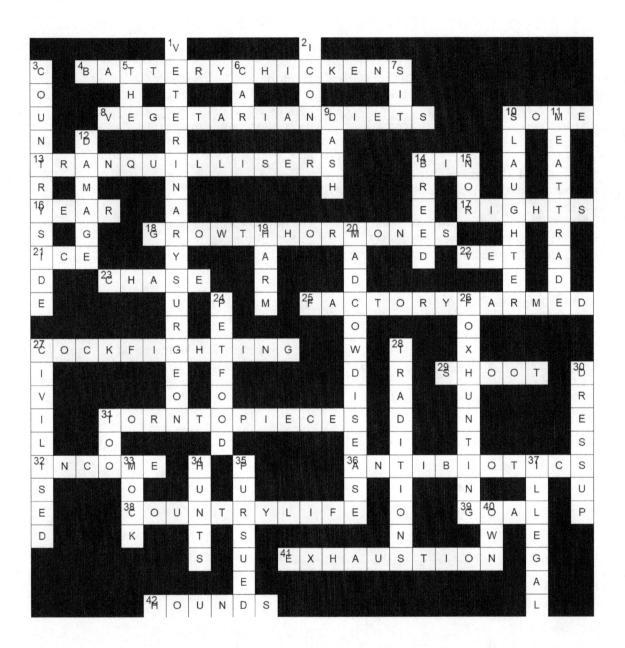

3. THE ARTS

3.1 Find the "odd one out".

[There may be more than one answer. Give your reasons.]

1.	A) a classic		B) a masterpiece		C) a work of art
2.	A) a loan		B) a grant		C) a subsidy
3.	A) opera		B) ballet		C) theatre
4)	A) modelling		B) sculpture		C) painting
5)	A) to appeal		B) to interest		C) to appreciate
6)	A) to stage		B) to screen		C) to put on
7)	A) galleries		B) museums		C) studios

3.2 Short text (see page 169 for comprehension questions)

The Arts cover an extremely wide **field**. They are encountered both in our education and leisure as we move from childhood to adulthood.

Painting, **sculpture** and **modelling** are usually met at an early age both as a form of play and at school where they provide release from reading, writing and arithmetic. **Literature** often appears in the form of bedtime stories. Many children's stories have become **classics**.

When children reach their teens, they generally develop an interest in **cinema**. For some this is mainly entertainment provided by Hollywood **blockbusters**, but others progress to more challenging films. Most school pupils read **novels** as part of **English Literature** and are also introduced to **Shakespeare**, though they are more likely to take an interest in **contemporary drama** as provided by television soap operas.

A visit to a music store will reveal a sizeable interest in **classical music**, especially among older people. **Opera** and **ballet** appeal to a minority of the population and are usually expensive both to **stage** and to watch.

3.3 Dialogue - read aloud in pairs

A: *In my view*, government money shouldn't be used to support the Arts.

3. THE ARTS

B: *I'm afraid I can't agree.* Public support for the Arts is the hallmark of a civilised society where people enjoy freedom of thought and expression.

A: *Those are very nice sounding words, but look* ...when we visit Art Galleries in other countries, we usually have to pay to go in, but when foreigners come to Britain, they're subsidised by the British taxpayer. They can enter the National Gallery and the British Museum without paying a penny.

B: *I think you're straying from the main point which is* the access of British people to their artistic heritage whether they're rich or poor. *If this also makes* Britain more attractive for overseas visitors, so well and good. *What's wrong with* creating a few more jobs in the tourist industry? *Think of* all the money that's spent in the souvenir shops of these galleries and museums.

A: *Well you might as well argue that* the government should subsidise all shops. *I'm saying that* it's the British taxpayer who pays the bill.

B: *You misunderstand me! I'm talking about* national institutions, centres of culture which represent the best of Britain's historical and artistic treasures.

A: *That's highly debatable.* Some of the exhibits you see from contemporary artists are no more than tins of baked beans or piles of bricks.

B: *I'm afraid you're just trying to prove a general point by quoting extreme examples. Of course, not every* artistic creation will be to everybody's taste. The Arts can never take new directions without risks. Both the impressionist painters and Picasso took risks.

A: *But in the real world*, if people want to take risks, they should do so at their own expense. They should either find private sponsors or sympathetic bank managers. *Why should other people* pay for the exhibition of junk which nobody wants?

B: *To come back to the main point, this isn't only about* contemporary, experimental art. *I'm talking about* the appreciation of great masterpieces which have been acknowledged for centuries.

3.4 Questions - discuss in pairs or groups

1. Do you think that the taxpayer should have to support the Arts? For example, why should a football fan have to pay for opera?

2. Does your country have any well-known artists who are famous for cinema, theatre, literature, ballet, opera, classical music or painting?

3. THE ARTS

3.   What are your "top three" art forms from the above list? Explain the reasons for your order of preference.

4.   In what ways were you encouraged to appreciate the Arts at home and at school? What jobs in the Arts world would be suitable for you?

5.   Give the names of your favourite novel, author, play, dramatist, film, film director, musical composition, composer, painting and painter. Why do you like them?

6.   Which country would you visit to appreciate the Arts? What would you plan to see?

7.   Do you think there should be greater or less censorship of the Arts in your country?

8.   How do you think technology has influenced the creation and consumption of art?

Dictionary reference

A classic: a work of art which is judged over a period of time to be of the highest quality and outstanding of its kind.

A masterpiece: a work of outstanding artistry, skill, or workmanship.

A work of art: an object made by an artist of great skill.

A loan: something lent on condition of being returned, especially a sum of money.

A grant: a sum of money given by a government or other organisation for a particular purpose.

A subsidy: money given as part of the cost of something, to help or encourage it to happen.

Opera: a dramatic work in one or more acts, set to music for singers and musicians.

Ballet: an artistic dance performed to music, using precise and highly formalised set steps and gestures.

Theatre: a collaborative form of performing art that uses live performers, usually actors or actresses, to present the experience of a real or imagined event before a live audience in a specific place, often a stage.

Modelling: making a representation of something, usually on a smaller scale.

Sculpture: the art of making three-dimensional representative or abstract forms, especially by carving stone or wood or by casting metal or plaster.

3. THE ARTS

Painting: a visual art, characterised by the practice of applying paint, pigment, colour or other medium to a solid surface commonly using a brush .

3.5 Crossword

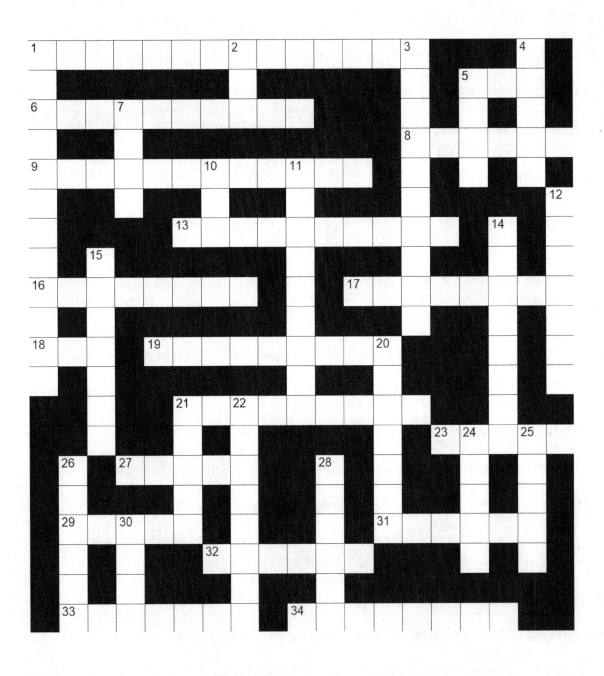

3. THE ARTS

Clues

ACROSS

1. Attracting a small number of people (8,6)
5. Tear (3)
6. Financial supported, usually by the government (10)
8. Repeat performance (6)
9. Art which attempts something new (12)
13. Enjoy (10)
16. Works of art presented to the public (8)
17. All that has been handed down from the past (8)
18. A period of time in history (3)
19. Rooms where pictures are displayed (9)
21. Serious music (9)
23. The opposite of liability (5)
27. Perform (5)
29. Containers for displaying flowers (5)
31. A person who is very small in height (6)
32. Swan Lake, for example (6)
33. Backing or help (7)
34. Creating a picture using oil or watercolour (8)

DOWN

1. Great works of art: paintings, for example (12)
2. Opposite of "no" (3)
3. Fiction: novels, plays and poetry (10)
4. Madame Butterfly, for example (5)
5. Solid mineral material found near the sea (4)
7. Appear (4)
10. Plan (3)
11. Precious things (9)
12. Places housing collections of objects, usually historical (7)
14. Great novels (8)
15. Cinema, theatre, opera, ballet, literature etc. (3,4)
20. Big pop concerts are sometimes held here (7)
21. In a _ _ _ _ _ of its own (5)
22. Something made by man (8)
24. To present a play in the theatre (5)
25. Soil (5)
26. Works of fiction, written in prose (6)
28. "Movies" in American English (6)
30. Liquid food with meat, fish or vegetable stock (4)

Crossword answer key

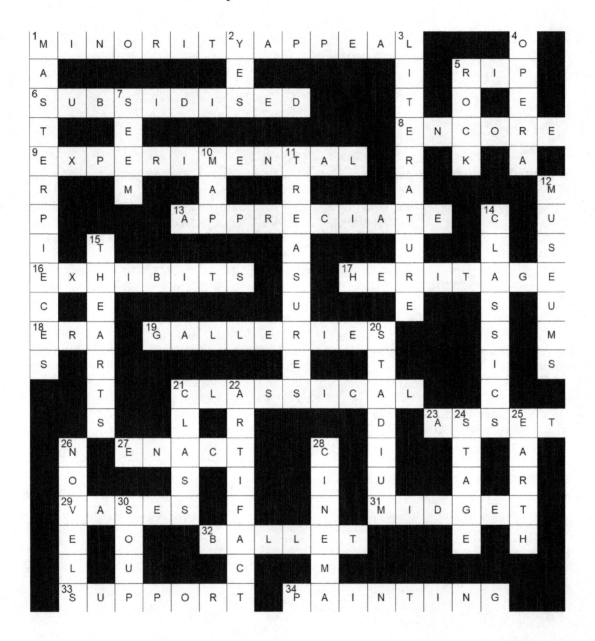

4. CRIME & PUNISHMENT

4.1   Find the "odd one out".

[There may be more than one answer. Give your reasons.]

1.	A) an offence	B) a crime	C) a sentence
2.	A) evidence	B) theft	C) proof
3.	A) capital punishment	B) corporal punishment	C) the death penalty
4.	A) to be fined	B) to be given a prison sentence	C) to be given a suspended sentence
5.	A) to deter	B) to discourage	C) to prevent
6.	A) a judge	B) a jury	C) a lawyer
7.	A) the defendant	B) the accused	C) the prosecution

4.2   Short text (see page 169 for comprehension questions)

The **legal process** in Britain can be illustrated by examining the **crime** of **shoplifting.** Every working day, small shops and large department stores have to protect themselves against this form of **theft**. Some stores display signs saying "WE ALWAYS **PROSECUTE THIEVES**", though their managers may have the option of warning **shoplifters** without reporting them to **the police**.

If a store manager decides to take a shoplifter to **court**, the legal process can be both time-consuming and expensive. The **lawyer for the prosecution** has to **prove** that the goods were deliberately taken and unpaid for. The **lawyer for the defence** may argue that **the defendant** was forgetful or suffering from mental illness. As evidence of non-payment, the manager may have to produce a till roll showing what purchases were made around the time of the **alleged** crime.

It is the task of the twelve members of **the jury** to listen to **the evidence** on both sides and to the **judge**'s **summing up**. They then **retire** to a separate room where they have to try to reach a **verdict**.

If the defendant is found **"not guilty"**, he or she is then **acquitted**. If a **"guilty"** verdict is **returned**, the judge will then **pass** sentence. The **sentence** for shoplifting may range from **a fine** or a **suspended** sentence for a first **offence** to a period of **imprisonment** for a persistent **offender**.

4.3   Dialogue - read aloud in pairs

4. CRIME & PUNISHMENT

A: *Do you think we should be* tougher on crime?

B: *Well, it depends on what you mean.*

A: *For example, we could* bring back the death penalty for murder, give longer prison sentences for lesser offences and lock up juvenile offenders.

B: Those really sound like Draconian measures. *Firstly, what do you do about* miscarriages of justice if you've already put innocent people to death?

A: *You'd only* use capital punishment *if* you were absolutely sure that you'd convicted the right person.

B: *But, there've been many cases of* wrongful conviction where people have been imprisoned for many years. The authorities were sure at the time, but later it was shown that the evidence was unreliable. In some cases, it'd been fabricated by the police.

A: *Well,* no system of justice can be perfect, *but surely there's a good case for* longer prison sentences to deter serious crime.

B: *I doubt whether they could act as* an effective deterrent while the detection rate is so low. *The best way to* prevent crime is to convince people who commit it that they're going to be caught. *It doesn't make sense to* divert all your resources into the prison system.

A: *But if* you detect more crimes, *you'll still need* prisons. *In my reckoning, if we could* lock up more juvenile criminals, *they'd* learn that they couldn't get away with it. Soft sentences will merely encourage them to do it again.

B: *Yes, but remember that* prisons are often schools for criminals. *To* remove crime from society, *you really have to* tackle its causes.

4.4   Questions - discuss in pairs or groups

1.   Should the death penalty exist as a punishment for murder or terrorism?

2.   Should the main purpose of prison be punishment or rehabilitation?

3.   What is the best way to deal with (a) joyriding (b) vandalism and (c) graffiti?

4.   Is it ever right for political activists to break the law?

4. CRIME & PUNISHMENT

5.   How strict should the law be with people who drink and drive?

6.   Which is the more serious problem in your country - tax evasion or social security fraud?

7.   Should the police have the right to stop and search you in the street without a warrant?

8.   Should the law respect the rights of homeless people to squat in unoccupied property or shop doorways?

9.   Should smoking cannabis be a criminal offence?

Dictionary reference

An offence: a breach of the law; an illegal act

A sentence: the punishment given to a defendant found guilty by a law court

Evidence: facts, information, etc that give reason for believing that something is true or present.

Theft: the action or crime of stealing.

Capital punishment: the state-sanctioned practice of killing a person as a punishment for a crime.

Corporal punishment: the use of physical force with the intention of causing some degree of pain, especially by hitting someone.

To be fined: to be charged an amount of money as a punishment for not obeying a rule or law.

A suspended sentence: a punishment served in the community rather than prison. If you break the conditions, you can be sent to prison.

Deter: discourage someone from doing something by instilling doubt or fear of the consequences.

Prevent: stop something from happening.

The defendant: an individual, company or institution sued or accused in a court of law.

The accused: a person or group of people who are charged with or on trial for a crime.

The prosecution: the side of a legal case which argues that a person who is accused of a crime is guilty.

4. CRIME & PUNISHMENT

4.5   Crossword

4. CRIME & PUNISHMENT

Clues

ACROSS

11. Declared to be the case (7)
12. Involve a defendant in a trial (4,2,5)
14. A period of time (4)
15. Period in history (3)
16. Opposite of "liability" (5)
17. Drop of water from the eye (4)
18. Idle; not hard-working (4)
19. One thing only (4)
20. Someone who has been a long time in prison; fail to keep up (3)
21. Minor crimes (6,8)
23. Accurate (4)
24. Grain or cereal crop (4)
25. To free (6)
26. Coming immediately after (4)
27. Payment to a lawyer or doctor for example (3)
28. Help! (3)
30. Quoted (5)
32. Of bright and clear weather (4)
33. An addition. 2+2 for example (3)
35. Siren of a car; part of a bull (4)
36. Untrue (5)
37. To attempt to prove a person guilty in a law court (9)
40. Extreme procedures (9,8)
42. To stop or seize by law (6)
44. To come back to give the verdict (6)
48. To kill (3,2,5)
50. Which came first - the chicken or the _ _ _? (3)
51. Try to heal or cure (5)
52. A means of preventing crime (9)
54. The lawyer for the accused (7)
55. The decision of the jury (7)
56. Stealing (5)

DOWN

1. Young criminals (8,9)
2. Conclusion (7,2)
3. The death penalty (7,10)
4. Discourage (5)
5. The administration of justice (5,7)
6. To administer the penalty (4,8)
7. The ultimate punishment (5,7)
8. To put behind bars (4,2)
9. Find guilty (7)
10. The lawyer trying to get a conviction (11)
13. To hand over a sum of money as a punishment (3,1,4)
22. Weak penalty (4,8)
29. Putting people in gaol (12)
31. The accused (9)
34. Wrongful conviction (11)
38. Not odd (4)
39. The twelve people who give their verdict (4)
41. Proof (8)
43. Strict (5)
45. To go to a private room (6)
46. A written record of the case (6)
47. No longer behind bars (4)
49. Deal with (6)
53. A smash and grab _ _ _ _ (4)

4. CRIME & PUNISHMENT

Crossword answer key

5. CULTURAL DIFFERENCES

5.1   Find the "odd one out".

[There may be more than one answer. Give your reasons.]

1.   A) similar   B) different   C) dissimilar

2.   A) a multiracial society   B) a multilingual society C) a monoculture

3.   A) immigrants   B) emigrants   C) migrants

4.   A) the Normans   B) the Romans   C) the Saxons

5.   A) to intermarry   B) to interfere   C) to integrate

6.   A) asylum   B) refuge   C) shelter

5.2   Short text (see page 170 for comprehension questions)

Most European countries have **multiracial societies** owing both to historical and geographical factors. Military conquests, persecution and economic hardship have all contributed to waves of **immigration**.

Early British history highlights the influence of the **Romans**, the **Vikings**, the **Saxons** and the **Normans**. More recently, we have opened our doors to **migrants** from **former colonies** as well as **refugees** seeking **political asylum**.

Racial integration has been successful in many areas of Britain. **Intermarriage** between people of **similar cultures** is now very common. The popularity of **Chinese** and **Indian food** and support for events such as the **Notting Hill Carnival** show a further acceptance of **cultural differences**.

However, good **race relations** have proved more difficult where there has been **large-scale immigration** involving **dissimilar cultures**, especially in areas of social deprivation - for example, where there is poor housing and high unemployment. Not only do **immigrants** become **scapegoats** for the problems of these areas, but they, themselves, may be reluctant to **integrate** for reasons of **religion** or **cultural identity**.

5.3   Dialogue - read aloud in pairs

A: *What do you think is the problem between* the English and the Americans?

5. CULTURAL DIFFERENCES

B: *That's a very interesting question,* because both nationalities share a common language and are usually on the same side in war-time, yet they rarely speak well of one another on a personal level.

A: *Are we talking about* a struggle for superiority?

B: *Yes, but* we measure our superiority in different ways. Ours is cultural and historical. We believe we're more civilised. We're the country of Shakespeare and the industrial revolution. Americans visit England in search of culture and history.

A: *So in what ways* are they superior?

B: *Well, obviously* in size. Everything's bigger - their country, their salaries, their roads, their companies. Theirs is the land of MacDonald's, Coca Cola, Microsoft and IBM. They enjoy telling us that they're the best.

A: *And are they right?*

B: Yes, if you measure success purely in dollars, *but there're two points here. Firstly,* many English people actually believe that "Small is Beautiful". They prefer countries where you don't get mugged in parks and subways.

A: *What's the other point?*

B: *I was coming to that.* It's the difference in character. *Maybe you think you're* the best in the world, but you don't go shouting about it from the rooftops. Americans lack our modesty and reserve. *They're probably* warmer and more friendly, but they're often very loud and extrovert *to go with it.*

A: *So you prefer* the British character?

B: *Not entirely. We tend to be* rather oblique in our conversation. When Americans speak, you can take them literally, but when English people speak *you have to read between the lines.*

A: *We say one thing and mean another?*

B: *Exactly.*

5.4   Questions - discuss in pairs or groups

1. "Cultural differences cause problems. It is better for people to stay in their own countries rather than to migrate to other ones." Do you agree?

2. Would you prefer to live in a monoculture or a multiracial society? Why?

5. CULTURAL DIFFERENCES

3. "It is better to study major international languages like English rather than to spend time on minority languages for the sake of regional identity." Do you agree?

4. "Governments should give regions in their countries more autonomy so that they can protect and enjoy their own cultures rather than serving the centralised policies of the capital city." Do you agree?

5. Is it better to marry someone of the same cultural background?

6. "Religion as a school subject should include all the major world religions - not only the majority religion in the country concerned." Do you agree?

7. What do you understand by the phrase "British Culture"? How does it differ from the culture of your own country?

Dictionary reference

Dissimilar: unlike or not the same

Multiracial: made up of, or relating to, people of several racial or ethnic groups.

A monoculture: a culture made up of a single social or ethnic group.

Migrants: persons who move from one place to another, especially in order to find work or better living conditions.

Normans: people of mixed Frankish and Scandinavian origin who settled in Normandy from about AD 912 and became a dominant military power in Western Europe and the Mediterranean in the 11th century..

Romans: people who lived in Rome or the Roman Empire between 625 BC and AD 476 who ruled over most of Europe.

Saxons: a group of Germanic people many of them who conquered and settled in much of Southern England in the 5th to the 6th centuries AD.

Intermarry: the act of marrying when the partners are from different ethnic, religious or social groups.

Interfere: try to control or become involved in a situation in a way that annoys other people because your involvement is not wanted or not helpful.

Integrate: mix with and join a social or racial group, often adopting its culture.

5. CULTURAL DIFFERENCES

Asylum: the protection granted by a state to someone who has left their country as a political refugee.

Refuge: a place of shelter where you are protected from danger or distress.

Shelter: a place giving temporary protection from bad weather or danger.

5.5   Crossword

5. CULTURAL DIFFERENCES

Clues

ACROSS
1. Communication between people of different origins (4,9)
8. Travel permits (7)
11. Becoming the spouse of a foreigner (13)
13. Winged creature living in heaven (5)
14. Opposite of imaginary (4)
16. Vast (5-5)
17. Notion or theory (4)
18. _ _ _ and drink! (3)
21. The opposite of similarity (10)
23. Clothing (4)
25. Lands belonging to a mother country (8)
29. Member of Germanic people who conquered parts of England in 500-600 AD (5)
30. A man-eating giant or terrifying person (4)
31. Short for telephone number (3)
32. Either .... _ _ (2)
34. A settler in a foreign country (9)
37. Opposite of off (2)
38. Origin of William the conqueror (6)
39. People sheltering from persecution (8)
41. To mix with other races (9)
42. A person's essential qualities or character (6)

DOWN
1. Coming together of people from different ethnic backgrounds (6,11)
2. Civilisation (7)
3. Bring up (4)
4. At a distance (4)
5. Coming to another country to live (11)
6. Tension (6)
7. A place of shelter for those in danger because of their beliefs (6)
9. Personality (9)
10. Large bird of prey, adopted as the symbol of the US (5)
12. With a mix of people from different lands (11)
15. Someone who works for a wage or salary (6)
16. To tell a fib (3)
19. After Christ (2)
20. People who are unfairly blamed (10)
22. Liberty (7)
24. A person of British or Northern European origin (5)
26. A circus entertainer who trains wild cats (4,5)
27. Who a person is (8)
28. Of Scandinavian origin, a long time ago! (6)
33. Julius Caesar, for example! (5)
35. Feel deep regret for a lost thing or dead person (5)
36. To be greatly and visibly worried (4)
40. European Currency Unit (3)

5. CULTURAL DIFFERENCES

Crossword answer key

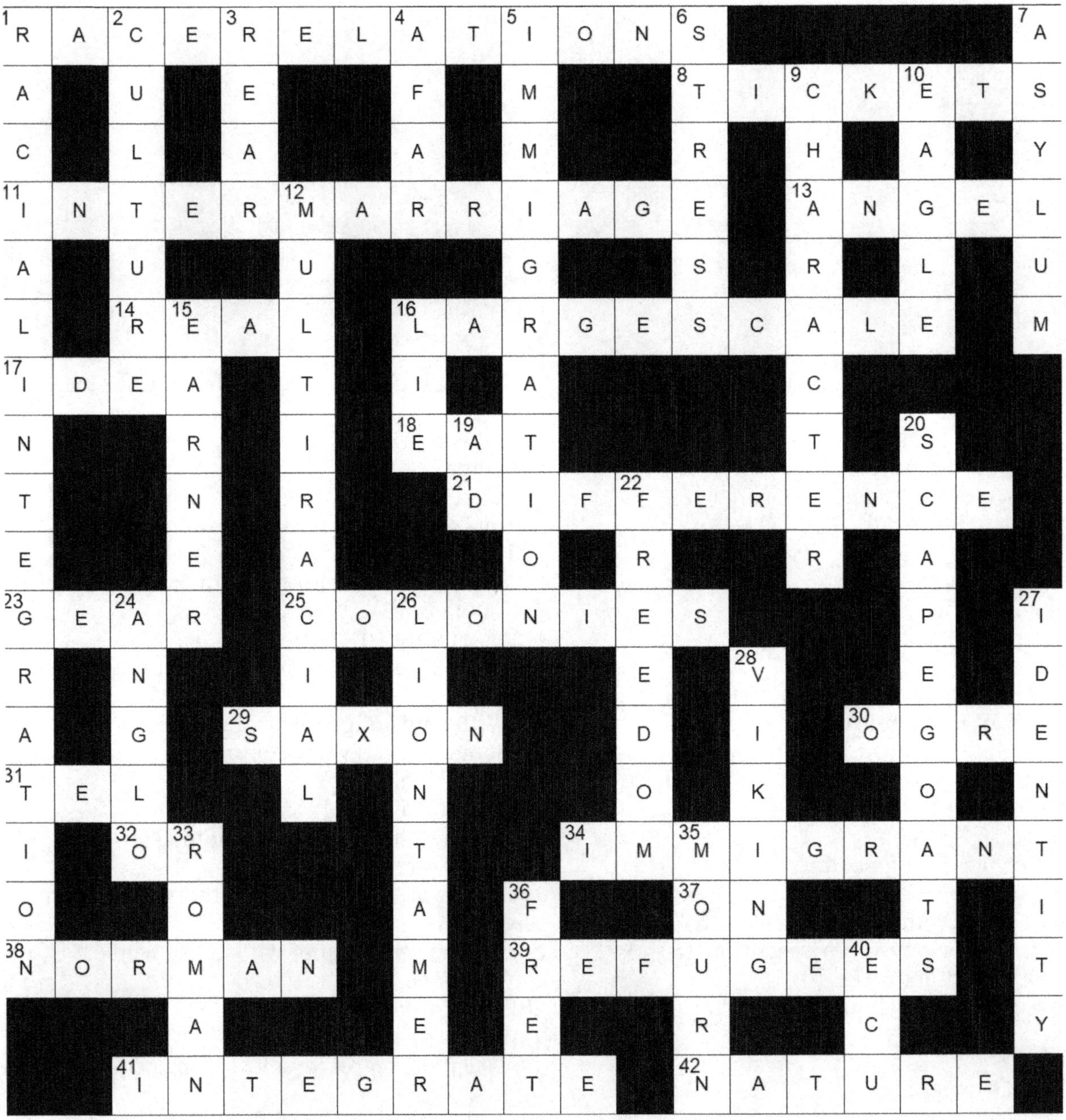

The completed crossword grid reads as follows:

Across / Down answers:

- 1. RACERELATION (R A C E R E L A T I O N S)
- 7. A / SSY... (down: A S Y)
- 8. TICKETS
- 11. INTERMARRIAGE
- 13. ANGEL
- 14. REAL
- 16. LARGESCALE
- 17. IDEA
- 18. EAT
- 21. DIFFERENCE
- 23. GEAR
- 25. COLONIES
- 29. SAXON
- 30. OGRE
- 31. TEL
- 32. OR
- 34. IMMIGRANT
- 36. F
- 37. ON
- 38. NORMAN
- 39. REFUGEES
- 41. INTEGRATE
- 42. NATURE

Down columns include:
- RACIAL (1 down)
- CULTURE / CLUB
- CREATION
- IMMIGRATE
- TRANS / CHAIR
- ETA
- SAY / ASSYLUM
- GRADE / GRADATE
- ANGER / ANGERNE
- VIK... (VI K O N)
- IDENTITY
- ORA / ROA
- MORE
- ONCE / OGEE

6. ECONOMICS

6.1 Find the "odd one out".

[There may be more than one answer. Give your reasons.]

1.	A) canals	B) railways	C) production lines
2.	A) protectionism	B) monopoly	C) free trade
3.	A) a consumer	B) a producer	C) a supplier
4.	A) labour-intensive	B) capital intensive	C) highly mechanised
5.	A) monetary policy	B) fiscal policy	C) economic policy
6.	A) skilled	B) manual	C) unskilled
7.	A) industrial	B) agricultural	C) manufacturing

6.2 Short text (see page 170 for comprehension questions)

Economic Theory, **Applied Economics** and **Economic History** provide the **social scientist** with wide areas of study.

Microeconomic theory is usually introduced through an examination of the principles of **demand** and **supply** and how prices are set under conditions ranging from **perfect competition** to **monopoly**. **Macroeconomics** operates on a larger scale and deals, for example, with models which governments may use in determining **monetary** and **fiscal policies**.

Course books in **Applied Economics** need to be revised frequently since this area focuses on the actual policies which have been implemented in recent years. These may include attempts to **control incomes**, to promote **regional development** or to **protect whole industries** from overseas competition.

British **Economic History** is an especially rich field since we claim to have had the first **agricultural** and **industrial revolutions**, to have pioneered the **canals** and the **railways** and to have been one of the most important **financial centres** in the world. The subject also explores the **conditions of the working class**, the **poor law** and early examples of **trade unions**.

6.3 Dialogue - read aloud in pairs

A: *Are you for or against* self-sufficiency?

6. ECONOMICS

B: *I definitely think that* countries should be self-sufficient in food and basic necessities.

A: *But that's impossible* in the modern world where countries have such large populations and economies are so interdependent.

B: *What I'm saying is that* we are too interdependent. Perhaps our populations are too big. *That's why I'm advocating* self-sufficiency as a goal.

A: *Then can you tell me what's wrong with* helping one another out. If Middle East countries which are covered with desert can earn money from oil production and if mountainous countries like Japan can export good cars, *why shouldn't they* import their food?

B: *Well, firstly we should ask if* they should be using up all that oil. Future generations could use less of it to reduce global warming. Does the world really need more and more motor cars. *How will* Japan sustain such a large population if countries decide to change direction?

A: *I expect that* Japan could adapt. It has a highly skilled workforce and a good technological base.

B: *That doesn't mean* it will switch its exports to products which the world really needs.

A: *Well, why should* Japan be self-sufficient in food then?

B: *You see, the alternative is* to buy food on the world market. *We all know that* when demand rises, so does the price. And when the price of food goes up, the poor countries which really need it are the last to afford it.

A: But many poor countries are food producers. *Surely, they can only benefit from* better prices.

B: The multinational companies which own the banana and sugar plantations *may* profit, *but very little* money is distributed to hungry people without jobs.

A: More demand should create a few more jobs!

B: *I doubt that* pay and conditions are very good. *Besides,* the production lines are often highly mechanised.

A: *Come off it!* Agriculture in developing countries is still fairly labour-intensive.

B: *Even so, not all* developing countries are food producers. The hamburger farms of those that are, make very wasteful use of the land and the profits go mainly to foreign investors. Very little is distributed to people who really need money to buy food.

6. ECONOMICS

6.4   Questions - discuss in pairs or groups

1. "Low tax, laissez-faire economies are better than ones with large public sectors." Do you agree?

2. "It is better to be within large economic unions like the European Community rather than outside them." Do you agree?

3. "Governments should legislate to prevent monopolies becoming too powerful." Do you agree?

4. "Free trade policies are always better than protectionist ones." Do you agree?

5. "Governments should not subsidise enterprises which are unprofitable." Do you agree?

6. "Countries should try to become self-sufficient in food and basic necessities." Do you agree?

7. "Giving financial incentives to companies which locate themselves in underdeveloped regions is a waste of public money. It is better to let them set up where they want to be." Do you agree?

8. "Increasing the minimum wage will encourage foreign investors to take their enterprises elsewhere." Do you agree?

Dictionary reference

Protectionism: government policies to restrict international trade to help domestic industries.

Free trade: a policy by which government does not discriminate against imports or interfere with exports by applying tariffs to imports or subsidies to exports.

Monopoly: a structure in which a single seller or supplier controls the market.

Labour-intensive: requiring a large number of workers.

Capital intensive: requiring a lot of investment in materials and equipment

Monetary policy: the action of a central bank or government of influencing how much money is in a country's economy and the cost of borrowing.

Fiscal policy: the use of government spending and taxation to influence the economy.

6. ECONOMICS

6.5   Crossword

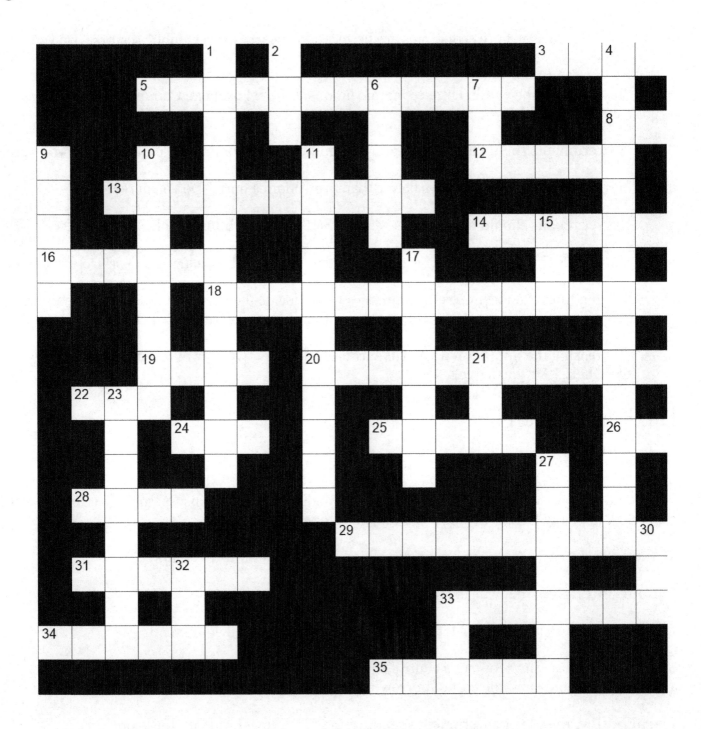

6. ECONOMICS

Clues

ACROSS

3. Decrease (4)
5. Rural - of the land (12)
8. Bachelor of Arts (2)
12. Relating to the economy as a whole (5)
13. Controlling the supply of money as the main method of stabilising the economy (10)
14. To have the means to buy (7)
16. Send abroad (6)
18. Relying on one another (14)
19. Single or only one (4)
20. Basic needs (11)
22. Income (3)
24. London School of Economics (3)
25. Dealing with individual commodities or producers (5)
26. Therefore (2)
28. The _ _ _ _ standard (4)
29. Done by machine (10)
31. Human resources (6)
33. In practice (7)
34. In principle (6)
35. The market for something (6)

DOWN

1. Safeguarding home industries through economic policy (13)
2. Take action (3)
4. Using many workers (6-9)
6. Have confidence in (5)
7. Target (3)
9. Weekly pay (5)
10. Control of the trade in a commodity or service (8)
11. Organised associations of workers (5,6)
15. Past tense of "feed" (3)
17. To derive advantage (7)
21. Polite form for addressing a man (3)
23. To be in favour of (8)
27. With a high level of ability (7)
30. Past tense of "do" (3)
32. Used for rowing (3)
33. An _ _ _ and a leg (3)

6. ECONOMICS

Crossword answer key

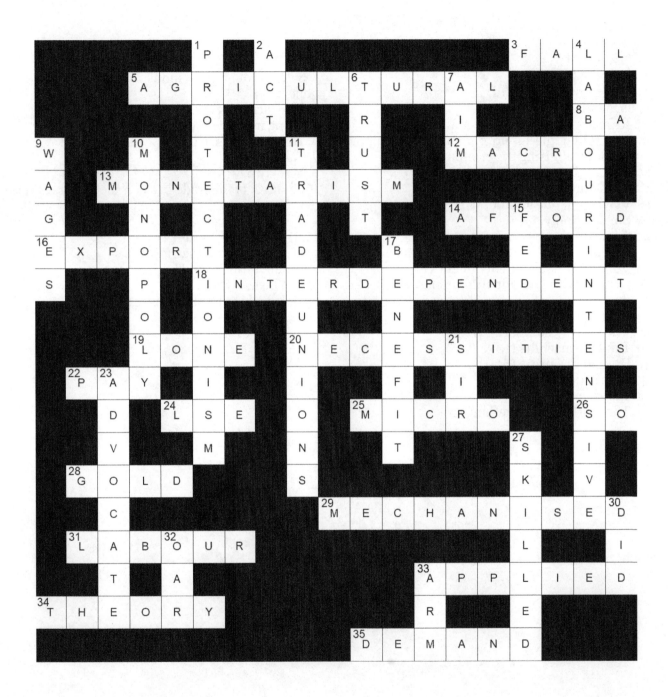

7. EDUCATION

7.1 Find the "odd one out".

[There may be more than one answer. Give your reasons.]

1. A) single sex   B) mixed   C) coeducational

2. A) compulsory   B) voluntary   C) optional

3. A) a state school   B) a public school   C) an independent school

4. A) nursery   B) primary   C) secondary

5. A) a grammar school   B) a comprehensive   C) a non-selective
                              school   school

6. A) streaming   B) mixed ability   C) ability grouping
                              grouping

7. A) continuous   B) final examinations   C) intelligence testing
        assessment

7.2 Short text (see page 170 for comprehension questions)

In Britain, school is **compulsory** between the ages of five and sixteen. **Primary** education continues until the age of eleven. Pupils wishing to enter **university** usually finish their **secondary** education when they are eighteen. Other types of **further** education are available for those who want to learn a **trade** such as catering or **specialise** at an early stage.

Over recent decades, the proportion of young people entering university has risen dramatically. The variety of degree **courses** on offer has also widened. It is now usual for students entering fields such as nursing to be based at university.

Educational terminology can be very confusing. For example, **preparatory** and **public** schools are **fee-paying** and both belong to the **independent** or **private sector**. **Middle schools**, which fall between primary and secondary education, are part of the **state system**, but do not exist in all parts of Britain.

Most state secondary schools are **"comprehensives"** and are **non-selective**. However, in some towns, institutions known as **grammar schools** operate **selectively**. Children are tested at the age of eleven and the bright ones are **creamed off**. Many parents argue that grammar schools should be abolished to allow **equality of opportunity** for all children. Others insist that a **fast track** is needed for **gifted pupils** and that diversity means more **freedom of choice**.

7. EDUCATION

7.3   Dialogue - read aloud in pairs

A: *What kind of* education would you choose for your child?

B: *For a start, it would have to be* a mixed school and not a boarding establishment.

A: *What have you got against* single sex schools?

B: *Clearly*, a coeducational environment promotes understanding between boys and girls. It's far more natural.

A: *Don't you think they* distract one another when they become teenagers?

B: *Well, maybe they do, but* they've got to learn to live together. I'm against all forms of segregation.

A: *How about* boarding schools? *Don't they* teach children how to live together? *I'd have thought they'd be* very useful for children without brothers and sisters.

B: *But* "only children" can still find friends in their neighbourhoods or local day schools. *Why have we got to* create large institutional families? If people decide to have children, then they should value family life.

A: *Would you prefer* your child to be educated privately or by the state?

B: *To be honest, that's a very difficult question, because if* the state schools in my town were very bad, *then* I might be tempted to pay private fees. I hope that wouldn't be necessary.

A: *Would you consider* sending your child to a grammar school?

B: *Again, that depends on the alternatives.* I prefer the comprehensive system, but *I wouldn't want* my child to be in mixed ability classes for all subjects. *There'd have to be some form of* streaming.

A: *What's wrong with* mixed ability teaching?

B: *The reality is that* people learn subjects such as languages and mathematics at different speeds. *It's a nonsense to* keep everybody at the same level *regardless of* their progress.

7.4   Questions - discuss in pairs or groups

1.   Would you prefer to send your child to a mixed or single sex school?

7. EDUCATION

2. Is day school always a better alternative to boarding school?

3. Should rich people be permitted to buy educational advantages by sending their children to private schools or should all schools be run by the state?

4. Do you prefer a system where children are put in fast and slow streams or is it better to create mixed ability classes?

5. Should school attendance be compulsory? What should be done to solve the problem of truancy?

6. Which system do you favour for measuring children's progress - final examinations or continuous assessment?

7. Do the "three Rs" (Reading, Writing and Arithmetic) make up the most important part of the school curriculum?

Dictionary reference

State schools: paid for by the government providing their pupils with free education.

Comprehensive schools: state secondary schools which do not select their pupils.

Grammar schools: state secondary schools which select their pupils through an exam.

Academies: publicly funded schools that operate independently of local authority control. They have more freedom over the curriculum, finances, and staffing than traditional state schools. They can be sponsored by businesses, universities, charities or religious organisations.

Independent schools: also known as private schools. These are not funded by the government and charge fees for tuition.

Public schools: expensive types of private schools that prepare pupils for top universities.

Special schools: these cater to pupils with special educational needs or disabilities.

Faith schools: these have a religious affiliation and may prioritise teachings of that faith within the curriculum. They can be either state-funded or independent.

International Schools: these cater to expatriate families or locals seeking an international education

Coeducational: having male and female students being taught together in the same school.

7. EDUCATION

Continuous assessment: a system of evaluating a learner's progress throughout a course.

7.5   Crossword

7. EDUCATION

Clues

ACROSS

5. Reasons for bad behaviour (7)
8. Programme of study in a single area (6)
9. Formal test (11)
12. National Extension College (3)
14. Type of school which chooses more able pupils (9)
16. Commander of the order of the British Empire (3)
18. Mixed (13)
19. Quick stream (4,5)
24. Polite phrase for less gifted pupil (4,7)
27. 2 + 2 =   (4)
28. English, History and Music, for example (4)
30. An electrically charged atom (3)
31. In the private sector (11)
33. A corpse (4)
35. Short for advertisements (3)
36. Private school for pupils going on to Public Schools (11)
37. Formal method of checking intelligence (2,4)
39. Higher (7)
40. Private - costing money (3,6)
43. Please reply (4)
46. System of fast, medium and slow lanes (9)
49. Broad programme of education (10)
50. Selective State Secondary School (7)
53. You have to do it (10)
58. A weak effort (4)
59. The director of a school (4)
61. A theory or notion (4)
63. Voluntary (8)
64. For both boys and girls (5)
65. The very best thing you can hope for (5)
68. The first stage of compulsory education (7)
69. Private school for elite aged between 13 and 18 (6)
70. Between Primary and Secondary (6)

DOWN

1. Calculations (4)
2. Staying late as a punishment (9)
3. Division (6)
4. For both the gifted and the less capable (5,7)
6. Monitoring performance all the time (10)
7. Type of state Secondary School for pupils who fail the selection test (9,6)
8. To select those at the very top (5)
10. Madame (3)
11. Government controlled (5)
13. Not compulsory (9)
15. Short for holidays (3)
16. For students from all kinds of backgrounds (13)
17. The verb "Etre" (2)
20. Measurement of academic performance (10)
21. How old you are (3)
22. A bad joke! (7)
23. To live as well as study in a school (5)
25. Noisy (4)
26. System for dealing with wrong-doers (10)
29. Being given the chance to do something (11)
31. Pictures (6)
32. Not state (7)
33. A wooden implement used for playing cricket (3)
34. Department of Social Security (3)
38. At a distance (4)
41. System of physical punishment (8)
42. Being given the same as other people (8)
44. Stage of compulsory education following Primary (9)
45. An upper class word for "homework" (4)
47. Type of education for those who need to catch up (8)
48. Talented (6)
51. A lively Scottish folk dance (4)
52. The smallest particle of a chemical element (4)
54. Opposite of "down" (2)
55. Opposite of "higher" (5)
56. Therefore (2)
57. Being able to select different schools (6)
59. Agreeable (5)
60. Exclude permanently from school (5)
62. An objective (3)
66. Not living in the school (3)
67. An old word for "yes" (3)

7. EDUCATION

Crossword answer key

8. ENVIRONMENT

8.1 Find the "odd one out".

[There may be more than one answer. Give your reasons.]

1.	A) green	B) efficient	C) environmentally friendly
2.	A) to conserve	B) to save	C) to protect
3.	A) to condemn	B) to campaign	C) to oppose
4.	A) traffic jams	B) motorway tolls	C) park and ride schemes
5.	A) nuclear energy	B) oil pollution	C) radioactive waste
6.	A) to ration	B) to share	C) to deplete
7.	A) sustainable	B) biodegradable	C) renewable
8.	A) an oil rig	B) a power station	C) a recycling plant

8.2 Short text (see page 171 for comprehension questions)

Greenpeace, Friends of the Earth and the Green Party all **campaign** for a **cleaner**, **healthier** and **less polluted** environment.

Greenpeace operates internationally and is able to embarrass governments and large oil companies through examples of **direct action** which attract public sympathy. These may include attempts to **block** the **disposal** of **radioactive waste** at sea or to **prevent** the **siting** of a new **oil rig**.

Friends of the Earth has branches in many towns and cities and is known especially for local initiatives such as opposition to **opencast coal mining**, **oil drilling** or **road-building schemes** and attempts to raise people's **awareness** of **green issues**.

The Green Party in Britain has been growing in popularity as more people acknowledge the climate emergency characterised by global warming and different forms of pollution. **The green movement** as a whole has had a significant influence on the agendas of the major political parties. The UK government has a range of policies aimed at 100 % reduction of **greenhouse gas emissions** from 1990 levels by 2050.

As more of our streets become **jammed up** with **cars** and more of our children suffer from **asthma**, the need for a **greener lifestyle** becomes inescapable.

8. ENVIRONMENT

8.3   Dialogue - read aloud in pairs

A: *What would be your favourite* green measure?

B: *I can answer that directly. I'd start by* rationing petrol to cut out unnecessary car journeys.

A: *What do you mean by* unnecessary?

B: *Let me explain.* Every morning, people go up and down motorways or cross from one side of town to the other in their cars, when they could quite easily take trains or buses.

A: *But* public transport is expensive and inconvenient.

B: It wouldn't be expensive if we could give it more public support. *Firstly*, motorists who want to live within their rations of normally priced petrol could leave their cars at home. Drivers who want more than their rations would have to pay a much higher rate for the extra. The profit could be used to develop environmentally clean vehicles and fast and efficient railway systems.

A: *Don't you think* you are being unfair to the private motorist and *what about* the car industry?

B: The private motorist is being unfair to the environment. *Why shouldn't those who* cause air and noise pollution do something to reduce it? *As for* the car industry, how many of our vehicles are truly British made? *Wouldn't it be better to* cut the import bill and turn our own production to electric vehicles?

A: *You can't* build new industries overnight.

B: *I'm not saying you can.* The oil companies are determined to get in the way of any scheme which means that people will consume less of their product. Many promising developments have been suppressed.

A: *Well, how is it all going to* change then?

B: *Only through* the election of a government which is courageous enough to take on the oil companies and ration petrol.

8.4   Questions - discuss in pairs or groups

1.   Does the environment belong principally to the human race?

2.   Do your consumption habits destroy the habitats of other species?

3.   Do you think that global warming is the main problem of our time?

8. ENVIRONMENT

4. Do you think that developers should be permitted to build big hotels and tourist complexes in the most beautiful places in your country?

5. Should the private motorist be made to pay more heavily through higher road tax, petrol prices, parking fees, congestion charges and motorway tolls?

6. Should cars be banned from city, town and village centres?

7. Is sustainable aviation fuel an honest attempt to improve the environment or an attempt to justify private jet travel?

8. Are you for or against nuclear power?

9. Does your country need stricter laws to punish noisy neighbours or discos which play loud music late at night?

10. Are your country's seas, rivers and lakes clean to swim in?

Dictionary reference

Environmentally-friendly: products or actions which are not harmful to eco systems.

Efficient: achieving maximum productivity with minimum wasted effort or expense.

Ration: restrict the supply by allowing each person to have only a fixed amount of a commodity.

Deplete: use up the supply (often used in relation to non-renewable resources).

Sustainable: causing little damage to the environment and therefore able to continue for a long time.

Renewable: relating to a natural resource such as solar energy, water or wood, that is never used up or that can be replaced by new growth.

Biodegradable: substances or objects capable of being decomposed by bacteria or other living organisms thereby avoiding pollution.

Sustainable Aviation Fuel: a replacement to fossil jet fuel, made from renewable raw materials such as feedstocks: cooking oil, plant oils, municipal waste, waste gases and agricultural residues. It is claimed that it can reduce greenhouse gas emissions by 80%.

Greenhouse gases: gases such as carbon dioxide, methane, nitrous oxide which cause global warming and climate change. They contribute to the greenhouse effect by absorbing infrared radiation.

8. ENVIRONMENT

8.5   Crossword

8. ENVIRONMENT

Clues

ACROSS
2. To conserve (4)
4. People who use land for new buildings (10)
8. Large deer (4)
10. Take care of (7)
12. Without the chemical Pb (4-4)
13. Solid material from which metal is extracted (3)
15. Women's Union (2)
17. Congestion i.e. traffic _ _ _ (3)
19. A gas used in crowd control (2)
21. To be more (9)
23. Productivity (6)
25. Vehicles carrying fare-paying passengers (6,9)
28. An alternative to electricity (3)
29. Large platform used for extracting petroleum (3,3)
32. Polluted fog (4)
33. Resistance or disagreement (10)
35. Zero (3)
37. A repeated sound (4)
38. Atomic power (7,6)
41. A layer of grass (4)
42. Understanding (9)
47. The indefinite article (2)
48. Coal or gas, for example (6,5)
50. A rare precious stone of purplish-red in colour (4)
51. Tall buildings (4-4)
52. Getting rid of nuclear waste (8)
53. A rest (3)
56. Egg-shaped (4)
58. A system of distribution other than price (9)
60. We do not own the earth; we just _ _ _ _ _ it! (5)
63. A plan (6)
66. Holiday villages (7,9)
67. Unwelcome sounds (5)
70. Elderly (3)
71. Save or protect (8)
72. Using again (9)

DOWN
1. Make better (7)
2. Locating (6)
3. Consume (3)
5. Panorama (4)
6. Leave your car and take the bus (4,3,4)
7. Small deer (3)
8. A period of time (3)
9. Black substance found in chimneys (4)
11. Programme of action (8)
14. European Currency Unit (3)
15. WWW or World Wide _ _ _ (3)
16. The address of a page on the WWW (3)
18. Charges for using fast roads (8,5)
20. A male deer (4)
22. A means of public transport (3)
24. Charge for leaving your car (7,3)
26. Unusable by-products of nuclear power (11,5)
27. Scheme (4)
30. Allergic respiratory disease (6)
31. A coniferous tree (6)
34. A nocturnal bird (3)
36. Way of living (9)
37. Surroundings (11)
39. Rodents found in sewers (4)
40. Prohibition (3)
43. A direction (3)
44. Productive with minimum waste (9)
45. A general fear, often without reason (5)
46. A theory that one event will cause a sequence of similar events (6)
49. To set free (7)
54. Contamination of the environment (9)
55. Means of keeping warm (7)
57. Car driver (8)
59. Environmentally friendly (5)
61. Assist (7)
62. Cut down on (6)
64. A person who censures (6)
65. Fossil _ _ _ _ (4)
68. A warning sign (4)
69. Help! (3)

8. ENVIRONMENT

Crossword answer key

9. FASHION

9.1 Find the "odd one out".

[There may be more than one answer. Give your reasons.]

1.   A) a catwalk   B) a promenade   C) a platform

2.   A) to consume   B) to market   C) to advertise

3.   A) to endorse   B) to condone   C) to promote

4.   A) a new look   B) a new design   C) a new image

5.   A) fashionable   B) in vogue   C) popular

6.   A) offensive   B) controversial   C) shocking

7.   A) a trend   B) a connection   C) an association

8.   A) glossy   B) artificial   C) colourful

9.2 Short text (see page 171 for comprehension questions)

Fashion forms a key part of many of our important industries, especially those involving **design**, such as **cars**, **household furniture** and **clothing**.

In the world of machines, **changes in design** often accompany technical improvements.

However, **new design** in clothing is more commonly motivated by fashion. Differences in the climate from season to season and the tendency to equate each new year with **a new look** provide textiles companies with frequent opportunities to renew their sales.

These **marketing** opportunities are often realised by associating products with people. **Fashion models** are highly paid to provide **appropriate images** of **good health**, **comfortable lifestyles**, **success** and **beauty**.

Fashion is usually regarded as **fun** and provides the focus of many **popular magazines**. However, controversy occurs in three instances. The image provided by the fashion model may shock, it may fail to have any connection with the product itself or it may **endorse a product** such as a fur coat which some people find offensive.

9. FASHION

9.3   Dialogue - read aloud in pairs

A: *In my opinion*, fashion is a complete waste of time, money and resources.

B: *I disagree entirely*. The world would be a very boring place without change.

A: Fashion doesn't only involve change. It's a very dishonest form of marketing based on artificial images which never translate into reality.

B: *But everyone understands that* the images are there to capture attention. People find them fun. *Haven't you ever* looked through a fashion magazine?

A: Only at the dentist's.

B: *What about* the glossy magazines which you get when you buy a Sunday newspaper? They're full of fashionable advertisements.

A: *That's true, but don't you think they're* a terrible waste of paper. *How many people* throw them straight into the dustbin?

B: A lot of people must read them and they don't add to the cost of the newspaper.

A: *There're two points here. Firstly*, the cost to the environment. *Think of all the* rain forests. *Secondly*, the advertiser may pay, but the costs are passed on to the consumer.

B: *That isn't strictly true*. If a company can sell in bulk, prices can be brought down. *You can't expect to* sell *unless* the consumer knows the product exists.

A: *I wouldn't mind* publicity *if* it told you something about the product, but by getting fashion models to market clothes and even cars, *you are hiding the truth*. When I buy clothing, I want to know if it's comfortable and how long it's going to last.

B: *That may be your reason, but some people* buy clothes because they want to look nice. *Perhaps they have* a special date or engagement. *People have always* liked dressing up.

A: *That may be so, but* traditional costumes were made to be worn more than once. *What worries me is* today's throw-away society where some people waste the world's precious resources while other people go without.

B: *Well I don't see why you should* blame the fashion industry for social injustice.

9. FASHION

9.4   Questions - discuss in pairs or groups

1.   Have you ever bought something because it was fashionable? If so, what?

2.   Does the fashion industry exist mainly to persuade people to spend money on things they do not really need?

3.   Is fashion selfish in a world where many people have not got what they need?

4.   Do you think fashion models should be used to sell products such as cars?

5.   Some fashion models refuse to advertise products involving animal cruelty such as cosmetics and fur coats. Would you buy such products?

6.   Would you like to be a fashion model if you were offered the opportunity?

7.   Is your country famous for any fashion products? Which ones? How are they marketed?

8.   Which countries have the best and worst fashions in clothes?

Dictionary reference

Catwalk: the runway at a fashion show on which models walk.

Promenade: a path for walking on, especially one built in view of the sea.

Platform: a raised level surface on which people can stand when they make speeches or give performances.

Endorse: make a public statement of your approval or support for something or someone.

Condone: ignore or accept behaviour that some people consider wrong.

Condemn: express strong disapproval.

Fashionable: popular or approved of at a particular time.

In vogue: the state of being popular or fashionable for a period of time.

Popular: liked, enjoyed or supported by many people.

Controversial: causing discussion, disagreement or argument.

9. FASHION

9.5   Crossword

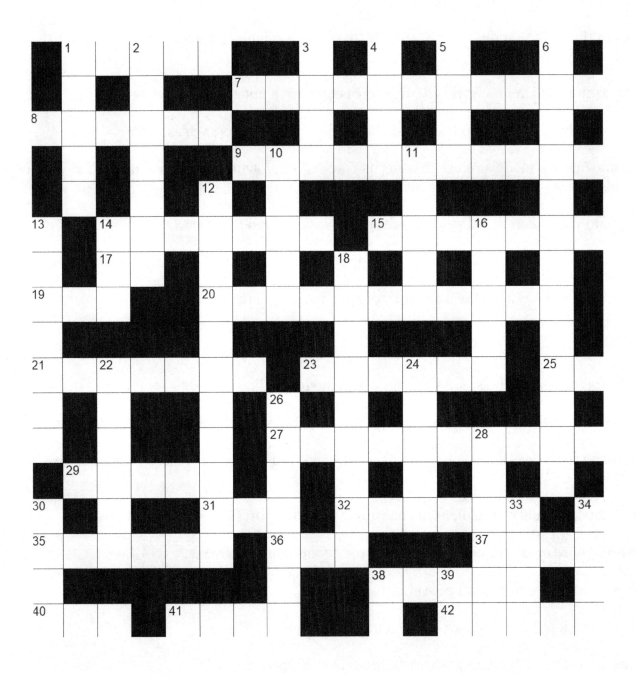

9. FASHION

Clues

ACROSS
1. Person who advertises new clothing (5)
7. Connection (11)
8. Shiny - describing magazines (6)
9. Suitable (11)
14. Opposite of kindness (7)
15. The latest style (7)
17. Preposition of place (2)
19. To trick or cheat (3)
20. In vogue (11)
21. To give approval (7)
23. Opposite of ugliness (6)
25. As a result (2)
27. Unnatural (10)
29. To burn off the tips of your hair (5)
31. To stitch (3)
32. Very dangerous (6)
35. People usually have five (6)
36. Youth and old _ _ _ (3)
37. Lovely! (4)
38. A special look (5)
40. To colour your hair (3)
41. In large quantities (4)
42. Places where birds live (5)

DOWN
1. Men (5)
2. To misrepresent (7)
3. Please answer (4)
4. Repeat sound (4)
5. Blond (4)
6. Shocking (13)
10. Small roads (5)
11. Without decoration (5)
12. Thinking of yourself and not of others (11)
13. Opposite of failure (7)
14. A tin (3)
16. Pastime (5)
18. Way of living (9)
22. Plan or pattern (6)
24. Not in good health (5)
26. Platform for fashion models (7)
28. Transformation (6)
30. Second hand (4)
33. Untruths (4)
34. Eleven in bingo (4)
38. A condition (2)
39. The indefinite article before vowels (2)

Crossword answer key

	¹M	O	²D	E	L			³R		⁴E		⁵F			⁶C	
	A		I			⁷A	S	S	O	C	I	A	T	I	O	N
⁸G	L	O	S	S	Y			V		H		I			N	
	E		T			⁹A	¹⁰P	P	R	O	¹¹P	R	I	A	T	E
	S		O		¹²S		A			L				R		
¹³S		¹⁴C	R	U	E	L	T	Y		¹⁵F	A	S	¹⁶H	I	O	N
U		¹⁷A	T		L		H		¹⁸L		I		O		V	
¹⁹C	O	N		²⁰F	A	S	H	I	O	N	A	B	L	E		
C				I			F				B		R			
²¹E	N	²²D	O	R	S	E		²³B	E	A	²⁴U	T	Y		²⁵S	O
S		E		H		²⁶C		S		N					I	
S		S		N		²⁷A	R	T	I	F	I	²⁸C	I	A	L	
²⁹S	I	N	G	E		T		Y		I		H		L		
³⁰U		G		³¹S	E	W		³²L	E	T	H	A	³³L		³⁴L	
³⁵S	E	N	S	E	S		³⁶A	G	E			³⁷N	I	C	E	
E					L			³⁸I	M	³⁹A	G	E		G		
⁴⁰D	Y	E		⁴¹B	U	L	K		F		⁴²N	E	S	T	S	

10. FOOD

10.1 Find the "odd one out".

[There may be more than one answer. Give your reasons.]

1. A) a cooker   B) a chef   C) a cook

2. A) boiling   B) cooking   C) cuisine

3. A) a course   B) a dish   C) a meal

4. A) convenience food B) fast food   C) frozen food

5. A) vitamins   B) proteins   C) carbohydrates

6. A) baking   B) roasting   C) frying

7. A) a hot plate   B) a grill   C) an electric ring

8. A) a bag   B) a basket   C) a trolley

10.2 Short text (see page 171 for comprehension questions)

Understanding an English **menu** depends not only on knowledge of particular **dishes**, but also on familiarity with **cooking techniques**. The key to these ways of preparing food is the **cooker** itself. Contrary to many students expectations, the cooker is not the person who prepares the food - that is the **cook -** but the **machine** used to supply **heat**.

Most cookers have four **hot plates**, usually situated on the **top surface**. Other names for hot-plates are **gas** or **electric rings**. These are used for **boiling, steaming, poaching, frying** and for making **chips**. Below the hot plates, you normally find the **grill** which delivers heat from above. **Grilled bacon** and **toasted bread** are commonly eaten for **breakfast** in Britain. Below the grill, is a chamber called the **oven** which is used for **roasting** and **baking**. A **roast potato** is **peeled** and **cooked in oil**, while a **baked potato** remains in its **jacket** and does not require any oil.

Some words on the menu assume more than one **process**. For example, a **mashed potato** is created first by boiling and then by **mashing -** crushing the **boiled potato** with a **fork**. Butter is usually added to give the final product a **smoother texture**.

10.3 Dialogue - read aloud in pairs

A: *What do you think of* British food?

10. FOOD

B: *That's a very difficult question to answer, because* if you look in two supermarket trolleys, you'll see that what people buy is completely different. Some people will go for fresh vegetables and wholemeal bread, while others prefer tins and packets of highly processed food.

A: Is there such a thing as British food?

B: That's the second problem, because a lot of what we buy comes from other parts of Europe or further afield. Many trolleys will contain both New Zealand butter and South African fruit.

A: *Well, what do people mean when they say* they don't like British food?

B: *I think it's probably possible to generalise about* what is eaten at main mealtimes. Northern Europeans, including the British, tend to eat more potatoes than Asians, who prefer rice.

A: *Can you explain why* many Asians prefer French or Italian cuisine to British cooking?

B: *That's both a question of* what different Europeans eat and how it's prepared. For example, pizza has become international. People are accustomed to eating it and Italians prepare it well.

A: Do the British prepare food badly?

B: *In fact,* we have some of the top chefs in the world, but only people with a lot of money experience British cooking at its best. Students staying in English families often have to put up with convenience foods, quick preparations served up by working couples who have little time for anything other than their jobs.

A: *Surely, not all* host families offer fast food.

B: *No* ....some are very careful about what they eat. They may buy brown rice, wholemeal bread, muesli and organically grown fruit. They may eat a mainly vegetarian diet. But this can cause different problems. Japanese students are used to eating white rice, while Southern Europeans are used to eating a lot of meat. Certain versions of the British diet are probably very healthy, but don't appeal internationally. *People simply aren't* used to them.

10.4   Questions - discuss in pairs or groups

1. "The government should make it more expensive for farmers to use pesticides and more profitable for them to grow organic food." Do you agree?

2. Which age group in your country eats most fast and convenience food? What could be done to encourage these people to eat more fresh food?

3. Should suppliers be permitted to irradiate fruit and vegetables to make them stay greener for longer on the shop shelves?

4. Do you think you can get all the nourishment you need from a vegetarian diet? Would you be happy to eat a vegetarian diet for a week?

5. The Hay diet encourages you to separate protein from carbohydrate, while the Chinese "Ying & Yang" diet encourages balanced eating. Can you describe any special diets which are followed in your country?

6. Should countries try to grow all their own food or is it better to depend on international trade to meet food needs?

7. Many people in Britain eat too much sugar, butter and salt. How healthy are eating habits (a) generally in your country (b) in your own family?

8. Are you for or against genetically modified food ?

Dictionary reference

Organic food: grown without the use of synthetic chemicals, such as pesticides and fertilisers, and does not contain genetically modified organisms.

Genetically modified food: organisms (plants or animals) in which the genetic material (DNA) has been changed scientifically (e.g. to help farmers prevent crop and food loss and control weeds).

Convenience food: food that has been pre-prepared commercially requiring minimum further preparation by the consumer.

Processed food: food that has been altered in some way during preparation: cut, chopped, washed, heated, pasteurised, cooked, canned, frozen, dried, dehydrated, mixed, packaged - anything done to it that alters its natural state. **Whole foods** are foods that have not been processed .

A diet: a special course of food to which a person restricts themselves, either to lose weight or for medical reasons.

Vegan : a person who does not eat or use any animal products such as meat, fish, eggs, cheese or other dairy products. A vegan diet is stricter than a vegetarian one which allows eggs and dairy products.

Vitamins: any of a group of natural substances that are necessary in small amounts for our bodies to develop and function normally.

Fats: nutrients in food that the body uses to build cell membranes, nerve tissue and hormones.

10. FOOD

Carbohydrates: substances that provide the body with energy such as sugar or starch.

10.5   Crossword

10. FOOD

Clues

ACROSS

1. Type of food which is easy to prepare (11)
6. _ _, was / were, been (2)
8. Italian dish with a large circular base (5)
10. Hot plate (4)
11. Money paid for service in a restaurant (3)
13. _ _, went, gone (2)
14. Mid morning snack (9)
15. To prepare food (4)
16. Short for "advertisement" (2)
17. A fresh-water fish (5)
21. Another word for "zero" (3)
22. Do you like your wine sweet or _ _ _ ? (3)
23. The first meal of the day (9)
25. Don't eat too much sugar if you want to stay _ _ _ _ ! (4)
26. An alternative to "coffee" (3)
28. Grown without the use of pesticides (7)
30. A healthy diet (8)
32. The roughness or smoothness (7)
34. Chemicals for killing insects and bugs (10)
37. Part of the cooker where toast is done (5)
38. Cooking with vapour above a saucepan on the hot plate (8)
40. Irish hot-pot (4)
43. Heating at 100 degrees celsius (7)
46. In good physical and mental condition (7)
47. Daily eating regime (4)
48. Small round green vegetable (3)
49. Strict vegetarian (5)
50. Not tinned or frozen (5)

DOWN

1. Ingredient which gives the body energy (12)
2. Person who doesn't eat meat (10)
3. Lovely! (4)
4. _ _ _ _ and saucers (4)
5. American for "Hello" (2)
6. Paper or plastic container (3)
7. Ready cut bread (6)
8. Italian speciality cut into different shapes (5)
9. VAT on British food is 0 % (4)
11. Mid to late afternoon meal (3)
12. A country famous for teas, spices and curries (5)
18. One gramme is a _ _ _ _ of weight (4)
19. A good cook must keep an eye on the _ _ _ _ (4)
20. To sample the flavour (5)
24. Cooking bread under the grill (8)
27. Attraction (6)
29. Cooking in the oven with oil (8)
31. A small insect often found in kitchens (3)
33. Spanish omelette (8)
34. Meat and soya are a rich source of this (7)
35. They kept us waiting a long time. The service was very _ _ _ _! (4)
36. This knife is too blunt. It can't _ _ _ (3)
39. A long slimy fish (3)
41. Most people have at least 3 a day (5)
42. The cook (4)
44. Part of the cooker for roasting and baking (4)
45. A wayside tavern (3)
46. Third Person Singular Masculine Subject Pronoun (2)

10. FOOD

Crossword answer key

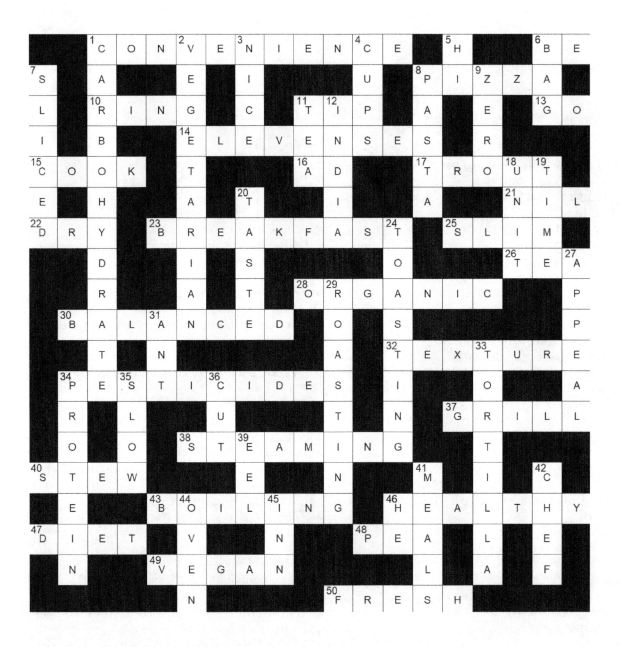

11. HEALTH

11.1 Find the "odd one out".

[There may be more than one answer. Give your reasons.]

1. A) a consultant   B) a surgeon   C) a doctor

2. A) to wound   B) to damage   C) to injure

3. A) a waiting list   B) an appointment   C) a consultation

4. A) to cure   B) to treat   C) to heal

5. A) to admit   B) to discharge   C) to transfer

6. A) a wheelchair   B) a bed   C) a trolley

7. A) a zimmer frame   B) a walking stick   C) crutches

8. A) homeopathy   B) massage   C) osteopathy

11.2   Short text (see page 172 for comprehension questions)

In major **emergencies** such as **road traffic accidents**, most people in Britain are **treated** under the **National Health Service**, known as **the NHS**. If you are badly **injured**, you will be taken by **ambulance** to **Accident and Emergency**. Once any **bleeding** has been **stemmed**, you will be **x-rayed** to see if you have **broken** any **bones**.

If you have **fractured** your **femur** or **patella,** you may be **operated on** by an **orthopaedic surgeon** fairly quickly. If you have done serious **damage** to your **pelvis**, you may need to be **transferred** to a large city hospital where **surgeons** specialise in **complex fractures** and **pelvic reconstruction.** Many unlucky motorcyclists require **specialist surgery** and often their legs are put **in traction** until they enter the **operating theatre.**

Soon after the **operation**, the **patient** is usually introduced to the **physiotherapist**. Some patients are put on a special machine which gently moves their **knee** and **hip joints**. If progress is maintained, they will be **mobilised** - moved from **bed** to **wheelchair** and then to **zimmer frame** or **crutches**. When they are walking on crutches, they will be taught how to climb steps. Providing their **surgical wounds** have **healed** and once they are no longer in **pain,** they can look forward to their **discharge** from **hospital**.

11.3   Dialogue - read aloud in pairs

11. HEALTH

A: *Would you ever consider* taking out private health insurance?

B: *I think it's a very sensible idea!*

A: But you are already paying for the NHS through national insurance. *Why should you have to insure yourself twice?*

B: *That's a very good question. The reality is that* the NHS covers people in major emergencies, but the service is under too much pressure to give adequate support.

A: *Can you be a bit more specific?*

B: *Certainly.* There're thousands of people who are in great pain. Some are waiting for minor surgery while others are waiting for treatment at pain control clinics.

A: But under the patients' charter, hospitals are meant to treat you within a certain time.

B: *Well, you know how they get round that one.* They make you wait for months before they put you on the waiting list.

A: *I don't think it's as bad as you make out. According to government statistics,* waiting lists are coming down.

B: *That may be true* for certain operations such as hernias where you're sometimes in and out of hospital within a day. They rush you through the system because they're short of beds. Then they hand you over to some elderly relative with a weak heart and expect them to look after you. They call it "care in the community".

A: But there're lots of back up departments such as Social Services and Occupational Therapy.

B: *Have you ever tried* contacting these departments and filling in their forms? Getting them to take quick action is virtually impossible.

11.4   Questions - discuss in pairs or groups

1.   "Governments should provide a first class National Health Service for everybody so that nobody would want to pay for private treatment." Do you agree?

2.   "Most nurses are overworked and underpaid." Do you agree?

3.   "People who have damaged their health through smoking or drinking should be at the back of the queue for expensive treatments." What do you think?

4. In your country, are waiting times long (a) to see a doctor (b) to have surgery?

5. "Alternative therapies should be recognised and licensed under the NHS to include
    (a) acupuncture (b) homeopathy (c) aromatherapy & massage (d) meditation (e) yoga (f)
    hypnosis and (g) faith healing." In which cases do you agree, if any?

6. "Western doctors prescribe drugs and medicines too freely since they do not have time to treat
    patients as individuals." Do you agree? Do you think other systems such as Chinese Medicine
    are any better?

7. How did the COVID-19 pandemic affect (a) school pupils and students, (b) people in
    employment, (c) senior citizens in your country?

8. What were the consequences and lessons of the COVID-19 pandemic in terms of education,
    employment, pressures on the health service (especially mental health) and political security?
    How well do you think your country coped?

Dictionary reference

Consultant: a person who gives professional or expert advice.

Surgeon: a doctor who is specially trained to perform medical operations.

Cure: restore to good health.

Treat: try to heal or cure.

Heal: cause a wound, injury or person to become healthy again.

Admit: allow someone to enter a place.

Discharge: allow someone to leave.

Homeopathy: a treatment based on highly diluted substances, which practitioners claim can cause the body to heal itself.

Osteopathy: a way of detecting, treating and preventing health problems by moving, stretching and massaging a person's muscles and joints.

Acupuncture: a treatment derived from Chinese medicine in which thin needles are inserted into the body at different locations and depths for therapeutic or preventative purposes.

Pandemic: a widespread occurrence of an infectious disease over a whole country or the world at a particular time. For example, **Covid 19**.

11.5 Crossword

11. HEALTH

ACROSS

2. Another name for alternative medicine (13)
11. Not "off" (2)
12. Rupture (6)
16. Spiritual cure (5,7)
19. Unit of electrical resistance (3)
20. National Health Service (3)
22. Not bright (3)
23. Look after (4)
24. Occupational Therapy (2)
26. Wooden or metal sticks giving leg support (8)
27. Noise of a cow (3)
28. Implement for cleaning floors (3)
31. Thigh bone (5)
36. Film showing bones (1,3)
37. Breast (3)
38. Foot doctor (11)
39. Not "hers" (3)
40. Provides strength (6)
42. Instead of a toilet, you may need a bed-_ _ _ (3)
43. Old English for "No" (3)
44. You have two on your upper body (4)
46. Saint (2)
48. Injured (4)
49. Schedule showing when patients will be treated (7,4)
50. Room in a hospital (4)
51. To cure (4)
52. Possessive adjective belonging to "me" (2)
53. Urgent problem (9)
54. Place where surgeons practise (9,7)
55. A night bird (3)
57. A married woman (3)
58. Knee cap (7)
60. Smashed (6)
63. A schedule telling you when it's your turn (4)
64. General Practitioner (6)
66. An arm and a _ _ _ (3)
69. Relating to bones and joints (11)
70. The plural of "is" (3)
71. Person who performs operations (7)
72. Anxiety or tension (6)
74. Release from hospital (9)
77. To give medical help (5)
78. Short for "laboratory" (3)
80. Vehicle for moving patients within a hospital (7)
81. To move someone from place to place (8)
82. A period of history (3)

DOWN

1. Deep cut in the body (5)
3. Not "on" (3)
4. Health care outside the NHS (7,9)
5. Miles Per Hour (3)
6. Phone (3)
7. To go quickly (3)
8. Holding a posture and reciting a mantra (10)
9. National Insurance (2)
10. Healing with small amounts of poisons (10)
13. The man with the ark (4)
14. Late stage of HIV infection (4)
15. Society (9)
17. Colour (3)
18. Massage using special oils (12)
21. Help offered through community agencies (6,8)
25. Preposition of motion (2)
29. Manipulation of the body through physical exercise (13)
30. Test (4)
32. Road Traffic Accident (3)
33. Chinese medicine (11)
34. Eastern practice of physical exercise (4)
35. Moving part of the body (5)
41. Vehicle used to take accident victims to hospital (9)
45. Apparatus which helps patients to balance and walk (6,5)
46. Not "Mono" but _ _ _ _ _ _ (6)
47. Broken (9)
48. Putting people in a trance (8)
50. Used for steering (5)
52. Iron is one (5)
56. Vehicle which allows patients to transport themselves (10)
58. Consumer of health care (7)
59. Metric measure for liquids (6)
60. British Telecom (2)
61. Programmes of study (7)
62. Place where family doctors work (7)
63. A _ _ _ _ with a view (4)
65. A person who runs (6)
67. A throaty noise involving liquid medicines (6)
68. Where most people spend the night (3)
71. A place where a building stands (4)
73. Do come in! Please _ _ _ down! (3)
74. Genetic material revealing your identity (3)
75. Help! (3)
76. Used for hearing (3)
79. British Airways (2)

11. HEALTH

Crossword answer key

12. HOLIDAYS

12.1 Find the "odd one out".

[There may be more than one answer. Give your reasons.]

1.	A) full board	B) half board	C) all-inclusive
2.	A) amenities	B) facilities	C) services
3.	A) operators	B) competitors	C) rivals
4.	A) hire	B) rental	C) purchase
5.	A) travel agents	B) timeshare developments	C) tourist complexes
6.	A) an itinerary	B) a journey	C) a route
7.	A) bed & breakfast	B) a hotel	C) a guest house
8.	A) a youth hostel	B) a tent	C) a caravan
9.	A) a tour	B) an excursion	C) a sightseeing trip

12.2 Short text (see page 172 for comprehension questions)

Although **travel agents** and **Tourist Information Centres** still exist in Britain and many other countries, the Internet is now the first choice for many people booking holidays.

Different choices of holiday accommodation have opened up following the rise of **air bed and breakfast,** a service which lets property owners rent out their spaces to travellers looking for places to stay. Similarly, there are websites and mobile apps for booking **flights, car rentals, guided tours** and **sightseeing excursions.**

You will still need to consider the **number in your party, the resort, the departure date, the duration,** the **type of accommodation,** the **eating arrangements (full board, half board** or **self-catering), travel** or **transport** options (e.g. **air or sea), car hire, equipment hire** (e.g. skis), **excursions** and **insurance cover.**

Budgeting forms an important part of most holiday plans. **Hotels** and **Guest Houses** can be **economical, medium-priced** or **luxury accommodation.** Money can be saved by making travel arrangements on **low cost airlines** well in advance. An **all-inclusive package holiday** may be the cheapest option, though you may wish to know whether your **investment** contributes to

12. HOLIDAYS

the **local economy** of your holiday resort, whether it brings **business** and **employment** to **local residents** or whether your presence merely helps to exclude them from the best parts of their own beaches.

Another important part of planning is what to do when you get there. A free-to-use **Artificial Intelligence** system such as ChatGPT can harness the whole power of the Internet in giving you suggestions and ideas. Just type in "Plan an itinerary for a 7-day trip to Lisbon" or "What is there to do in Lisbon when it rains?" and the system will surprise you with its detailed responses.

12.3   Dialogue - read aloud in pairs

A: *What do you think of* package holidays?

B: *Well,* they're usually very cheap, but joining a crowd of noisy people and eating plastic food *is not my idea of* a holiday.

A: Are the resorts worth visiting?

B: Some of them are, *but in my experience it's better to* arrange private accommodation *rather than* accepting the tour operator's choice of hotel.

A: *But surely,* you can see what you're getting on the website or in the holiday brochure.

B: *You may* see a picture of the hotel and *there may even be* a popular beach, but if you want to go to a nicer locality, you can spend all day getting there.

A: Then *how do you go about* making your own arrangements?

B: *It's not as difficult as you think.* Go to the website of a booking agency or a low-cost airline and there you can reserve the "flight only". Booking in June or mid September avoids the school holidays, but there's still a good range of flights then and prices aren't too high.

A: How do you find private accommodation?

B: *That's very easy.* Just search "Holiday Lets" together with your holiday destination and your search engine will return a number of booking sites for holiday homes and apartments. *However,* remember to check the availability of transport, especially if you don't drive.

A: *Surely,* there will be bus services.

B: *There are two problems here.* Some of these homes are a long way from bus routes. *Moreover,* bus services can disappear altogether when the tourist season comes to an end. Many resorts are like ghost towns from October to May.

12. HOLIDAYS

12.4   Questions - discuss in pairs or groups

1. Do you prefer to book an all-inclusive package or to make your own holiday arrangements?

2. Which form of accommodation did you have on your last holiday? Were you satisfied with it?

3. What are the advantages and disadvantages of TWO of the following forms of holiday accommodation?

   (a) five star hotel   (b) budget hotel   (c) guest house
   (d) bed & breakfast   (e) self-catering villa   (f) farmyard cottage
   (g) ocean liner   (h) student family   (i) youth hostel
   (j) caravan   (k) tent   (l) canal boat

4. Which form of accommodation would you prefer for your next holiday and how many people would you like to accompany you?

5. What are your favourite holiday activities?

6. Describe your best and worst holiday.

7. Have parts of your country been spoilt by tourist developments?

8. A friend wants to get to know your country and is planning a tour. What advice would you give about places to visit, travel, accommodation, eating out, shopping, sightseeing, things to bring and souvenirs to buy?

Dictionary reference

Full board: includes bed, breakfast, lunch and evening meal.

Half board: includes bed, breakfast and evening meal (no lunch).

All-inclusive package: travel, accommodation, food, excursions and entertainment.

Timeshare: a holiday property with shared ownership. You share the cost of the property with other buyers and receive a guaranteed amount of time in it every year.

Amenities: something that helps to provide comfort, convenience or enjoyment.

Facilities: buildings, equipment, or services provided for a particular purpose.

12. HOLIDAYS

12.5   Crossword

12. HOLIDAYS

Clues

ACROSS

4. Insurance (5)
5. Up-market B & B (5,5)
9. French for "me" (3)
10. Everything and everybody (3)
11. Amenities (10)
13. Phantom resort (5,4)
14. Roof features, triangular in shape (6)
17. Canal boat (5)
18. Mobile home (7)
20. European Community (2)
21. Rival company (10)
22. Transport from airport to holiday destination (8)
24. Nothing (3)
25. Sister of your father or mother (4)
29. Apparatus (9)
30. Don't forget to turn it off before going on holiday (3)
31. An arrangement (4)
32. Periodical (7)
33. You may see one in the fields in the spring (4)
39. To gamble on an outcome or result (3)
40. Plane journey (6)
41. Prospectus (8)

DOWN

1. All meals and accommodation (4,5)
2. The definite article (3)
3. Neither too dear nor too cheap (6-6)
4. A bedroom on a ship (5)
6. Looking at the local attractions (11)
7. The opposite of "plus" (5)
8. Short for "mother" (2)
12. Way or itinerary (5)
15. Cheap (10)
16. Place for tents (8)
19. Customer (6)
23. hire charge (6)
26. Money paid to secure the booking (7)
27. Not far (4)
28. Length of holiday (8)
33. Large ship for cruising (5)
34. The youngest member of the family (4)
35. Your best friend (4)
36. Invoice (4)
37. Sightseeing trip (4)
38. A famous computer company (3)

12. HOLIDAYS

Crossword answer key

13. LANGUAGE LEARNING

13.1 Find the "odd one out".

[There may be more than one answer. Give your reasons.]

1.	A) first language	B) second language	C) native tongue
2.	A) English	B) Esperanto	C) Chinese
3.	A) grammar	B) vocabulary	C) pronunciation
4.	A) look and say	B) audio-lingual	C) grammar-translation
5.	A) fluency	B) accuracy	C) proficiency
6.	A) a lesson	B) a course	C) a lecture
7.	A) a dictionary	B) a lexicon	C) a thesaurus
8.	A) motivation	B) memory	C) aptitude

13.2 Short text (see page 172 for comprehension questions)

Recent **psycholinguistic studies** on how people learn **languages** have been accompanied by emphasis among **English language teachers** on **the learner** as an individual. **Preferred learning styles** are increasingly respected and **learner independence** is encouraged. For some teachers, **non-interference** is the key to giving a successful **lesson**. For others, this is an abdication of **the teacher's role** and shows ignorance of what can be done to make learning more efficient.

If there has been a **revolution in language teaching methodology**, surely there are some things teachers can do to help learners.

In the past, many of Britain's top schools modelled the teaching of **modern languages** on the teaching of Latin. **Oral fluency** was therefore undervalued and **accuracy** in the **written language** became the main goal. Your French might be excellent on your school report, but you could still arrive in France and fail to understand a word.

A separate **method** known as **audio-lingualism** made its appearance in **private language schools**. This emphasised the **primacy of the spoken word,** yet **lesson content** was mainly **structural** and contained few of the **features of spoken English** used as a vehicle for **communication**. Surely teachers can at least provide learners with good **models of target behaviour.**

13. LANGUAGE LEARNING

13.3   Dialogue - read aloud in pairs

A: *Which should be* the official world language - English or Esperanto?

B: *In my opinion, there's only one choice* - English!

A: *But that's not a neutral choice. Think of* all the advantages English-speaking countries have. *Not only* do you save money by not having to learn a second language, *but* you can make a lot of money by teaching your native tongue. *Besides*, the choice of a European language is unfair to people from other continents.

B: *Actually*, Esperanto is closer to European languages than any others.

A: *But at least it's* culture-free. With Esperanto as the world language, no country would be accused of exporting both its language and its culture.

B: *Well, I'm not sure whether* you can really separate language from culture. The two have developed alongside one another. One would be very impoverished without the other.

A: *That may be true, but then* you're inviting political conflict. *Who is going to decide whether* North American culture is superior to Chinese culture?

B: *Nobody really has to decide. All you really have to do is* to see which language is already being used for international business, trade and political negotiations. That language is English.

A: *It doesn't mean that the situation will be the same in the future.* China could well emerge as the world's strongest economy.

B: *That may be so, but* the economic strength of Japan hasn't led to much teaching of Japanese. *You also have to consider* the vast size of the knowledge base available to English speakers - academic research, scientific reports and an infinite number of books and periodicals.

A: Much of that knowledge base has already been translated.

B: *I doubt that* many other languages can match the size of the English dictionary, especially any single Chinese dialect. *Look how* many languages have had to borrow from English, for example, computer terms such as ESCAPE and RETURN.

A: But English has borrowed from the Romans, the Vikings, the Saxons and the French.

B: *Yes, but* over a long period of history. Besides, these borrowings illustrate the both the breadth and flexibility of the English language. *You just can't begin to compare* Esperanto with English as a tool for communication.

13. LANGUAGE LEARNING

13.4   Questions - discuss in pairs or groups

1.   Describe "the good language learner" according to the following criteria: (a) woman or man, (b) old or young, (c) extrovert or introvert, (d) other characteristics, (e) habits, (f) motivation and interests.

2.   In what ways are you a good or bad language learner?

3.   How many languages can you speak and how well can you speak them?

4.   "Fluency in a language is more important than accuracy." Do you agree?

5.   Are you satisfied with the way languages are taught in your country?

6.   Do tourists often try to speak your language when they visit your country?

7.   "Every child should learn to speak a second language." Do you agree?

8.   Which should be the official world language -   English or Esperanto?

Dictionary reference

Native tongue: the language of the country where someone is born.

Esperanto: an artificial language made by combining features of the main European languages. It is intended to be both easy to learn and international.

Grammar-translation: a method of language teaching where the learner translates from their own language into the target language and learns and memorises grammatical rules and how they apply to sentences translated between the two.

Audio-lingualism: a method of language teaching which involves a drill routine of listening and speaking and which aims to promote habit -formation through repetition of basic patterns.

Notional-functional approach: a method of language teaching which focuses on the communicative meanings of words and expressions, similar to what is now called **the communicative approach**.

Proficiency: one's competence in speaking a particular language.

Fluency: the ability to speak a language smoothly and without hesitation to a near native level.

13. LANGUAGE LEARNING

Accuracy: how correct a speaker's use of language is including their grammar, pronunciation and vocabulary.

13.5   Crossword

13. LANGUAGE LEARNING

Clues

ACROSS
1. Post Script (2)
3. "I went" but "did you _ _?" (2)
8. An ancient Scandinavian language (5)
9. Rendering from one written language to another (11)
11. Reference book listing words by theme or topic (7)
12. For example (2)
13. "Does it have" or "has it _ _ _?" (3)
14. Getting one's meaning across to other people (13)
17. The definite article before French nouns in the feminine singular (2)
18. Oxygen (3)
19. To put in order of preference (4)
20. Help (3)
23. Faith (6)
25. First language (6,6)
28. The answers to the exercise (3)
29. Without reference to a country's civilisation and society (7-4)
32. Small error (4)
33. Metal container (3)
34. To get back (6)
36. Used for hearing (4)
37. No, you can't. Yes, I _ _ _ (3)
39. Relating to hearing (5)
41. Meaning (5)
45. Movement (6)
47. To permit (3)

DOWN
2. Relating to form (10)
3. Short for "grammatical" (4)
4. Takes the place of a noun (7)
5. To communicate (8)
6. Study of how people learn languages (17)
7. IQ (12)
10. Invariable or uncountable (3)
15. Relating to the spoken word (4)
16. Lacking in resources (12)
21. Also (3)
22. The opposite of "strengthening" (9)
24. Used for seeing (3)
25. Names of things (5)
26. Reference book grouping words with similar meanings (9)
27. Ability to speak without hesitation (7)
30. Latin for "work" (4)
31. Ability to remember words and rules (6)
35. Practice in the _ _ _ of English (3)
38. Gossip (4)
40. An untruth (3)
42. Smoking or _ _ _-smoking (3)
43. Girl's name, short for Emile (3)
44. Neither... _ _ _ (3)
46. Transitive (2)

13. LANGUAGE LEARNING

Crossword answer key

14. MALE & FEMALE ROLES

14.1 Find the "odd one out".

[There may be more than one answer. Give your reasons.]

1.	A) a babysitter	B) a homemaker	C) a breadwinner
2.	A) prejudice	B) harassment	C) discrimination
3.	A) racism	B) political correctness	C) sexism
4.	A) the chair	B) the chairperson	C) the chairman
5.	A) a husband	B) a wife	C) a partner
6.	A) Ms	B) Mrs	C) Miss
7.	A) crèches	B) nurseries	C) primary schools
8.	A) capabilities	B) talent	C) qualifications

14.2 Short text (see page 172 for comprehension questions)

In the British General Election in 1997, some of the most powerful men in the country lost their seats to **professionally successful women**. 119 women were elected to the House of Commons and 5 women secured Cabinet posts. By 2024, there were 226 female MPs out of a total of 650 members and 7 women in the cabinet. Although the number of **small businesses** run by women has also increased, it is still less than one third of the total.

Many women leave corporate life because of their difficulties in progressing in large organisations, especially in the world of finance, where men are generally favoured for the top managerial posts.

During the twentieth century, women in Britain had to **campaign** vigorously for **equal rights**, the **right to education**, the **right to vote** and the **right to work** in posts traditionally reserved for men. It was largely through **war work** that women proved their **capabilities**. More recently, they have been **outperforming** men in public examinations. **Women's rights** campaigns have focused particularly on language and thought. Terms such as "**chairman**" have been changed to more neutral descriptions such as "**chair**" or less ambiguous alternatives such as "**president**". This is part of the recent concept known as "**political correctness**".

Some men are careful to avoid accusations of **sexism** and **sexual harassment** while others have reacted by campaigning for "**men's rights**".

14. MALE & FEMALE ROLES

14.3 Dialogue - read aloud in pairs

A: *What kind of rights* do women and men want in your country?

B: *To begin with*, most women and men want the right to work.

A: *Do you think* both partners in a relationship should expect to work in times of high unemployment?

B: *It's often an economic necessity for* both partners to work, especially if they're buying a house or providing for a family.

A: *What if there isn't* enough work to go round?

B: Then some people will be out of a job - they could be either women or men.

A: *Aren't they more often* women?

B: *Yes, but it isn't that* women don't want to work. *For a start*, they suffer more discrimination in the work-place. When a young woman applies for a job, it isn't possible to ask her whether she intends to start a family or not, but it is possible to give the job to a man with fewer qualifications.

A: *Does that happen?*

B: *Perhaps not as much as it used to*, but if a woman leaves a job to start a family, it may be very difficult for her to return to full-time work. Many women are in part-time jobs and on very low rates of pay. Underemployment of well qualified women who are doing unchallenging work is a huge waste of talent.

A: Are there many underemployed men?

B: *Yes, certainly.* There are those who do seasonal work and those who depend on cash in hand for occasional jobs.

A: *How about* unemployed men?

B: Well, unemployment can be very frustrating for those men who believe that they should be the bread-winner in a relationship. Many live on state benefits. There is also a group of men who have not had a job in years. Lack of work experience can make a person unemployable.

14.4   Questions - discuss in pairs or groups

14. MALE & FEMALE ROLES

1. How have traditional gender roles changed during your lifetime? What has influenced these changes?

2. In your country, do women generally have equal opportunities in the work-place e.g. the same pay and promotion opportunities as men?

3. Is it easy for people to continue their careers after taking time off work to start a family? Do companies provide crèches or nurseries?

4. What provision does the state in your country make for child care?

5. Do parents and teachers in your country encourage girls and boys to grow up differently? Do girls and boys generally (a) play with the same toys (b) participate in the same sports (c) choose similar courses of study at school and university?

6. Do you think women and men should perform the same or different roles? Are men usually the bread-winners and women usually the home-makers in your country?

7. How does language use reinforce gender stereotypes? What can be done to challenge gender norms within educational institutions and the media?

Dictionary reference

Breadwinner: the member of a family whose whose salary or wages provide the main means of support.

Homemaker: the person who spends their time looking after a home or doing housework instead of being employed outside the home.

Prejudice: an unfavourable opinion formed beforehand not based on knowledge, thought or reason.

Discrimination: to treat someone unfairly, especially on the basis of ethnicity, age, sex or disability.

Harassment: repeatedly behaving in a way which makes someone else feel scared, distressed or threatened.

Gender stereotypes: preconceived ideas about the traits and behaviours members of a certain gender do or should display.

Gender norms: current ideas about how women and men should be or act.

Political correctness: the act of avoiding language and actions that could be offensive to others, especially those related ing to sex, gender and race.

14. MALE & FEMALE ROLES

14.5   Crossword

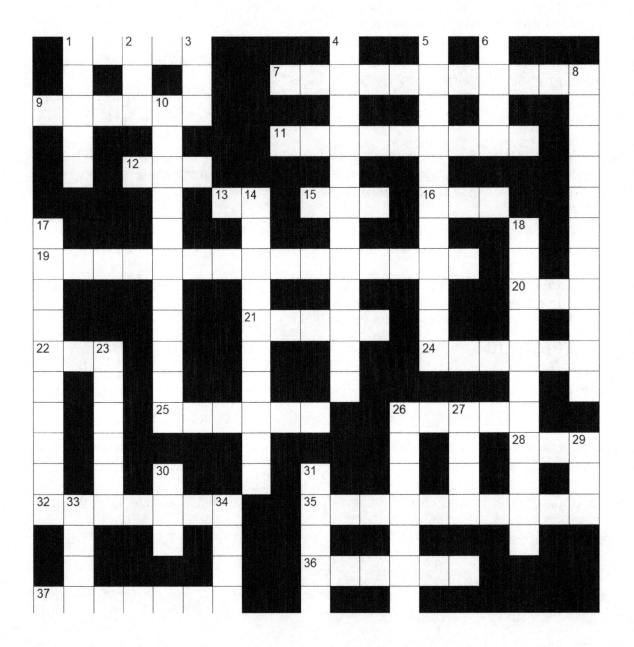

82

14. MALE & FEMALE ROLES

Clues

ACROSS

1. Eve's gift to Adam (5)
7. Ideas about how women or men should be or act (6,5)
9. The course of one's working life (6)
11. Someone who does housework instead of going to work (9)
12. Mother (3)
13. Political correctness (2)
15. Beer or real _ _ _ (3)
16. Marry (3)
19. Not having enough work to do (15)
20. Adam's partner (3)
21. A sum of money offered dishonestly in return for a favour (4)
22. A small, supernatural creature common in German folklore (3)
24. To go back to a previous state (6)
25. Discrimination by men against women or conversely (6)
26. To rest on water without sinking (5)
28. The opposite of "no" (3)
32. Husband and wife (7)
35. Troubling someone or annoying them repeatedly (10)
36. Day care for young children provided by the work-place (6)
37. Either member of an established relationship (7)

DOWN

1. Change to fit new situation (5)
2. Apple _ _ _ and custard (3)
3. Make a mistake or do the wrong thing (3)
4. Describing someone who would never be given a job (12)
5. A person who earns the money to support a family (11)
6. A formal expression of choice by means of a ballot (4)
8. A woman seeking the right to vote through organised protest (11)
10. Common entitlements (5,6)
14. What one can do (10)
17. To achieve more than someone else (10)
18. Widely held but oversimplified ideas (11)
23. To prefer (6)
26. Money (7)
27. Used for rowing a boat (4)
29. Come in. Please _ _ _ down (3)
30. Pelvic joint (3)
31. A sudden upsetting or surprising event (5)
33. A two dimensional space (4)
34. An affectionate form of address (4)

14. MALE & FEMALE ROLES

Crossword answer key

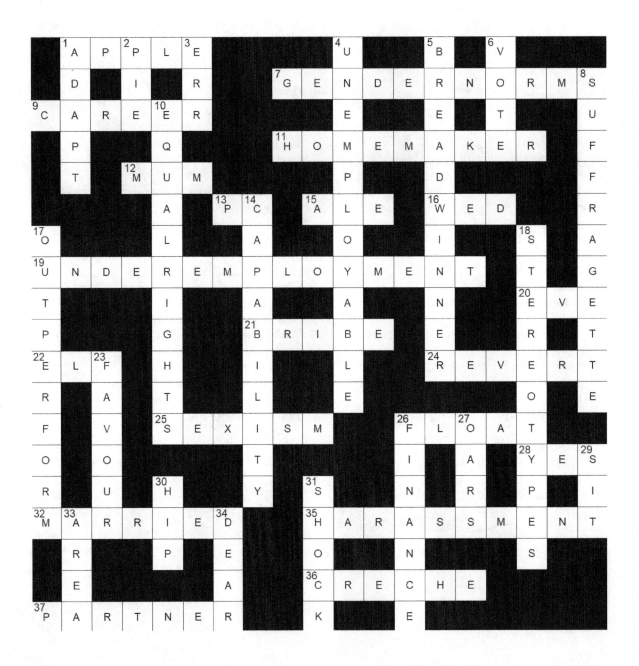

15. MARRIAGE

15.1 Find the "odd one out".

[There may be more than one answer. Give your reasons.]

1.	A) marriage	B) cohabitation	C) trial marriage
2.	A) monogamy	B) bigamy	C) polygamy
3.	A) a commitment	B) a contract	C) an agreement
4.	A) compatibility	B) security	C) stability
5.	A) divorce	B) separation	C) remarriage
6.	A) a couple	B) a partner	C) a spouse
7.	A) a ceremony	B) a reception	C) a honeymoon

15.2 Short text (see page 173 for comprehension questions)

Britain has one of the highest **marriage** and **divorce** rates in Western Europe. The average age for **first marriages** is now approximately 28 for men and 26 for women. Nearly 40% of British marriages are **remarriages** where one or both **partners** have already been **divorced**. The average age when divorces occur is about 39 for men and 36 for women. For the **Anglican** and **Catholic** churches, marriage is for life, but for between one third and a half of British **husbands** and **wives**, marriage is for about ten years.

Nearly a third of British **babies** are born outside marriage and about half of these are born to **couples** with **stable relationships** living at the same address.

Attitudes towards different kinds of relationships have become far more liberal in Britain in recent decades. **Cohabitation** has become far more acceptable and some ministers of the Church of England are even prepared to marry people who have already been divorced. Many couples appreciate the atmosphere and **symbolism** of a **church wedding**, though others prefer the simplicity and honesty of a **registry office**. In other words, they attach little or no importance to the **religious aspect** of marriage, although they may still want a **legal contract**.

15.3 Dialogue - read aloud in pairs

A: *What are the advantages and disadvantages of getting married? Don't you think it's better to stay single?*

15. MARRIAGE

B: *Well, if you ask me, it all depends on your circumstances.*

A: *What do you mean?*

B: *I mean that* people's situations can be very different. *Let's take the very extreme situation of* a young woman who marries an old man as an example.

A: *Tell me more!*

B: The old man might be very rich, *though on the other hand* he could be very talented. *As for* the young woman, she may have a lot in common with the old man; *alternatively*, she may be interested in his money.

A: *What are you trying to say?*

B: *To come to the point*, there are so many different motives for marriage that *it's impossible to generalise about why people* prefer married to single status.

A: *Rubbish!* It must be possible to compare living together with someone to living on your own. *What about the question of* independence?

B: *But you don't seem to realise that* many married people live totally independent lives.

A: *That may be so*, but *for most people the whole point of* marriage is to live together and possibly to raise a family. *That's what this discussion's about.*

B: *In that case, it's obvious that* children are a commitment for life. *I guess that* many single people have different priorities *or else* they believe that they would make unsuitable parents.

A: *Surely,* there's more to marriage than having children.

B: *If you're talking about* the religious or security aspects of getting married, the divorce rate is so high in Britain that these don't seem to be relevant any more. *Why not just* stay single. You can still live together with other people for as long as you find them compatible.

15.4   Questions - discuss in pairs or groups

1.   Are you for or against trial marriages i.e. living together outside marriage to test your compatibility?

2.   Do you think that marriage should be for life? Should divorce be made easier or more difficult?

15. MARRIAGE

3. Why do you think that the divorce rate has become so high in Britain and many other countries?

4. Is it better to marry someone of the same educational, social, cultural and racial background?

5. Is it better to marry someone of approximately the same age? Where marriage is between a man and a woman, should the man be older than the woman?

6. How important is the religious aspect of marriage to you and to people generally in your country? Which aspects are more important, if any?

7. What are the advantages and disadvantages of arranged marriages compared to love marriages?

8. How do modern attitudes towards marriage differ from those of previous generations in your country?

Dictionary reference

Cohabitation: a legal term applied to living together and having a sexual relationship without being married.

Monogamy: a relationship with only one partner at a time rather than multiple partners.

Polygamy: marriage to more than one spouse at a time.

Bigamy: the crime of marrying a person while still being legally married to someone else.

A commitment: a promise , obligation or firm decision to do something.

A contract: a written or spoken agreement, especially one which is legally enforceable.

Spouse: a person's husband or wife.

Partner: either member of a married couple or an established unmarried couple.

Predict: say what you think will happen in the future.

Convey: express a thought or a feeling so that it is understood by other people.

Compatibility: how people get along; existing together successfully.

Stability: being steady without ups and downs; the ability to withstand stress.

15. MARRIAGE

Security: freedom from fear, anxiety, danger or doubt; a sense of safety or certainty.

15.5   Crossword

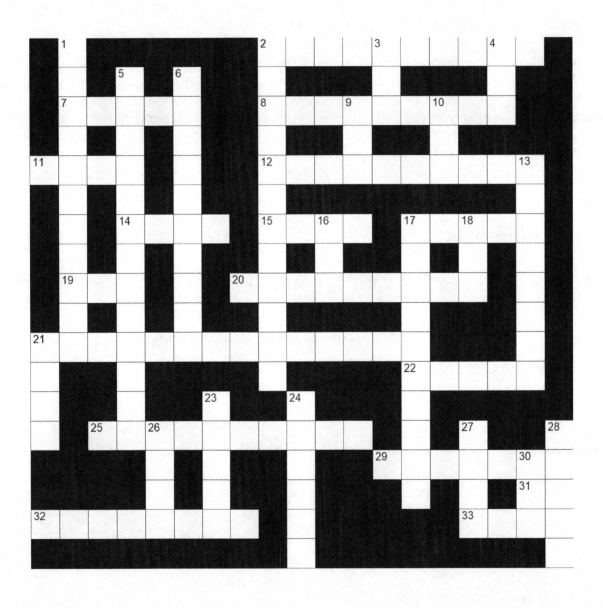

15. MARRIAGE

Clues

ACROSS

2. Going well together (13)
7. Sixth astrological sign in the zodiac (5)
8. Holiday following a wedding (9)
11. Two dimensional space (4)
12. Man about to be married (10)
14. Best friend (4)
15. To try out (4)
17. To start (5)
19. Oxygen (3)
20. A state without ups and downs (9)
21. Place where couples can marry lawfully without a church ceremony (8,6)
22. Better safe than _ _ _ _ _ (5)
25. Formal decision to part company (10)
29. Termination of marriage (7)
31. Automobile Association (2)
32. Unmarried woman (8)
33. Not "his" (4)

DOWN

1. Proportion of marriages ending in divorce (7,4)
2. Living together (12)
3. Some or _ _ _ (3)
4. Local Area Network (3)
5. Living together experimentally before real marriage (5,8)
6. Responsibility (10)
9. Opposite of beginning (3)
10. Used for rowing (3)
13. Having only one married partner (8)
16. To cry (sob)
17. Assistant to the bride (10)
18. Homosexual (3)
21. Worn by the bride at the moment when she becomes a married woman (4)
23. Woman about to be married (5)
24. Being married to two partners at the same time (6)
26. Small green round vegetables (4)
27. Upper class (4)
28. Beauty and the _ _ _ _ _ (5)
30. Automobile (3)

15. MARRIAGE

Crossword answer key

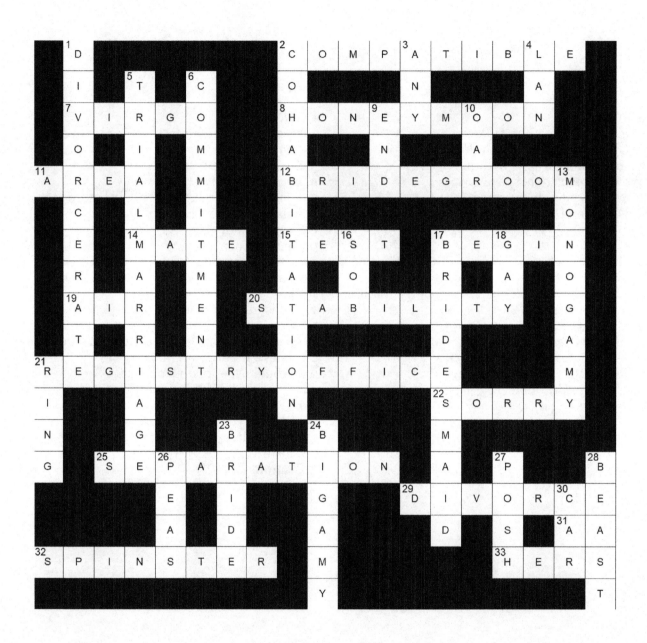

16. THE MEDIA

16.1   Find the "odd one out".

[There may be more than one answer. Give your reasons.]

1.	A) a broadsheet	B) a journal	C) a tabloid
2.	A) aerial	B) satellite dish	C) cable
3.	A) a channel	B) a station	C) a wavelength
4.	A) advertising revenue	B) the licence fee	C) road tax
5.	A) to screen	B) to stage	C) to broadcast
6.	A) circulation	B) readership	C) audience rating
7.	A) to censor	B) to curb	C) to regulate
8.	A) a business tycoon	B) a media mogul	C) a press baron

16.2   Short text (see page 173 for comprehension questions)

The media includes national and local **newspapers**, free to air and subscription **tv channels**, public and commercial **radio stations**, **magazines**, **journals** and **websites** on the Internet.

Traditionally the support of the owners of **national newspapers** was important to political parties hoping to get elected. 90% of the UK-wide **print media** is still owned and controlled by just three companies. However, newspaper **circulation** has been in decline as both television and the Internet offer a more visual style in delivering news. Now social media platforms such as Facebook, WhatsApp, YouTube and Instagram play an increasingly important part in getting messages across.

In a true democracy, the media would provide **accurate information** and would **protect the interests** of all the people. However, many **media platforms** are largely dependent on **advertising** for their **revenue**. Although they are often provided free to **viewers** and readers, the **controllers** and **editors** have to please the **advertisers**.

Viewers and readers are **classified** by both **media providers** and **advertising agencies** according to different **social categories** ranging from grades A and B for **senior managers** and **professional people** through to grades D and E for **unskilled workers** and **casual labourers** respectively.

16. THE MEDIA

16.3   Dialogue - read aloud in pairs

A: *Do you think the Government should act to* curb the power of media barons who own newspapers, tv channels and digital platforms such as Facebook and X?

B: Yes, but no Government would risk too much confrontation. Good or bad publicity decides election results.

A: *But that's terrible! Are you saying that* foreign-based multinationals decide who is going to be British Prime Minister.

B: *Yes and no. There's no doubt that* these large monopolies have a great deal of power. *On the other hand*, Britain is fortunate to have public corporations such as the BBC which get their income from the licence payer rather than advertisers.

A: *Why do you say* we're fortunate when we have to pay over £150 per year for just seven TV channels and a handful of radio stations?

B: Because this money can be used to make programmes which people really want to watch or listen to. The BBC isn't owned by anybody and doesn't have *to bow to the wishes of* large advertising agencies.

A: *Well*, it may not be owned, but it is controlled by a Board of Governors appointed by the Prime Minister. *Don't you think that there's a danger of* self-censorship?

B: *What do you mean by that?*

A: *I mean that* people who want to get on in the BBC may be tempted to choose programme content which pleases the Director General and the Government. If the Director General allows too much criticism of the Government, then the Home Office could retaliate by reducing the licence fee.

B: *I doubt that this would ever happen.* The BBC prides itself on its independence, and Government interference of this kind would be too obvious. Journalists and politicians of integrity would find a way of publicising the truth. Electorates can usually tell when censorship and corruption have reached a certain level.

A: *You mean, you can't fool all of the people all of the time?*

B: *Exactly.* Even the media barons have to switch their allegiance when they find they're backing the wrong horse. *People just won't continue to accept* editorial lines, for example on schools or the health service, which don't match up with their experience. A fall in viewing figures or readership *would damage the pockets of our masters!*

16. THE MEDIA

16.4   Questions - discuss in pairs or groups

1.   In Britain, tabloid newspapers, which contain a lot about celebrities sell many more copies than serious newspapers. Is this the case in your country?

2.   Do reporters and photographers respect the private lives of famous people in your country? How much freedom should the press be allowed by law?

3.   Is the media in your country mainly owned by a few large monopolies? Should the law allow ownership of several newspapers, TV channels or social media sites?

4.   Is there a bias towards any particular political party or interest group in your country's media?

5.   Which do you prefer (a) TV channels without advertising paid for by a licence fee or (b) Free TV channels paid for by advertising?

6.   In Britain, there are restrictions on what can be screened on TV before 9 p.m. Do you think that TV programme content should be censored?

7.   Should young children be free to access social media sites on the Internet?

8.   Should smart phones be allowed in school classrooms?

Dictionary reference

Broadsheet: a newspaper printed on large sheets of paper, generally believed to be more serious than tabloids.

Tabloid: a newspaper with a compact page size focusing on sensational news stories.

Journal: a newspaper that deals with a particular subject or professional activity.

The licence fee: the fee paid in the UK for watching television, which funds the BBC.

Circulation : the public availability, for example - the number of readers or viewers.

Censor: examine books, plays, news reports, films etc and to cut out parts considered to be offensive or unsuitable.

Media mogul: an individual who owns a significant share of the news, film or television industry.

Press baron: a person who owns several newspapers and controls what they publish.

16. THE MEDIA

16.5 Crossword

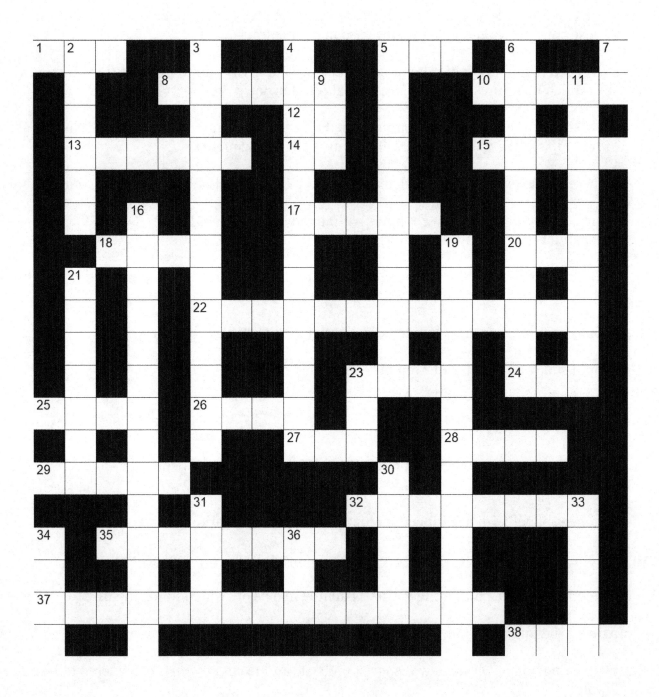

16. THE MEDIA

Clues

ACROSS

1. How old a person is (3)
5. To pull or to _ _ _ the line (3)
8. A warning in Latin (6)
10. Cuts (5)
12. How do you _ _? (2)
13. The viewing surface of a television (6)
14. Opposite of "out" (2)
15. A long wooden seat (5)
17. Break or shatter (5)
18. Small car or short skirt popular in the 1960s (4)
20. Hostel (3)
22. The politics of a newspaper (9,4)
23. A long narrow aperture for something to be inserted (4)
24. An alternative to electricity (3)
25. Cosy (4)
26. To go round and round (4)
27. Rupert Murdoch's satellite channel (3)
28. To limit or stop (4)
29. TV, radio, newspapers, the internet, the arts etc. (5)
32. The popular press (8)
35. Listeners (8)
37. The boss of the BBC (8,7)
38. See Saw _ _ _ _ (4)

DOWN

2. Frivolous talk (6)
3. Receiver for broadcasts from space (9,4)
4. Transistor wavelengths (5,8)
5. Earth TV (11)
6. Publicity (11)
7. As white _ _ snow (2)
9. A heavy weight (3)
11. BBC1 BBC2 ITV CH4 (2,8)
16. Number of people who watch a TV programme (7,7)
19. Prejudice favouring one Party (9,4)
21. Income for advertising or the licence fee (7)
23. Utter (3)
30. Broadcast through optical fibre wire (5)
31. A _ _ _ _ of beer, please! (4)
33. A portion (5)
34. Past tense of "make" (4)
36. A tooth-like part of a wheel in a machine (3)

16. THE MEDIA

Crossword answer key

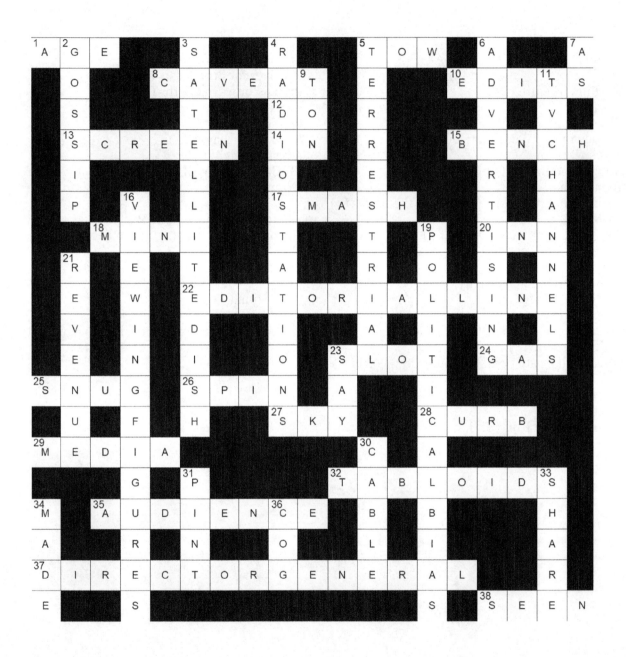

17. POLITICAL SYSTEMS

17.1   Find the "odd one out".

[There may be more than one answer. Give your reasons.]

1.   A) Conservative   B) Liberal Democrat   C) Tory

2.   A) Green   B) Labour   C) Socialist

3.   A) The Leader   B) The Prime Minister   C) The Government
         of the Opposition

4.   A) Parliament   B) The Commons   C) The Lords

5.   A) a publican   B) a monarchist   C) a republican

6.   A) The Cabinet   B) The Home Secretary   C) The Chancellor

7.   A) benefits   B) subsidies   C) welfare

17.2   Short text (see page 173 for comprehension questions)

In Britain, the three main political parties are the **Conservatives**, the **Socialists** and the **Liberal Democrats**. The Conservatives, also known as the **Tories**, occupy **the right.** The Socialists, also known as the **Labour Party** are traditionally associated with **the left**. The **Lib Dems** are seen as the stepping stone between the Tory and Labour parties, though they have far fewer **Members of Parliament**.

Most of the political power belongs to the **House of Commons**, the **elected chamber** of the **British Parliament**. The power of the **House of Lords**, the **second chamber** is very limited and the role of **the monarch** is largely symbolic.

General elections must be held within periods of five years, though **Prime Ministers** can choose the date they consider to give them the best chance of **reelection.** Britain is divided into **650 parliamentary constituencies** each represented by an elected **MP** (Member of Parliament). The party which returns the largest number of MPS usually forms **the Government**, while the party with the second largest number of **seats** becomes **the Opposition**. One of the first tasks of a new Prime Minister is to choose the team of ministers which will head important Government **departments**. These form **the Cabinet.** The key posts are the **Chancellor of the Exchequer** and the **Foreign & Home Secretaries.**

17.3   Dialogue - read aloud in pairs

17. POLITICAL SYSTEMS

A: *Do you think that* the class system still exists in Britain...*I mean,* is there an upper, middle and working class?

B: *Well, I think* the terminology is a bit out of date. *You see,* many top managers regard themselves as workers. *That said, there's definitely* a group of people who are disadvantaged and you'll find some of them living on welfare benefits such as universal credit.

A: Do they have jobs?

B: Yes, many of them do, but their pay is rarely much more than the minimum wage. *It's a scandal,* because many pizza parlours, pubs and burger bars are really being subsidised by the Government.

A: *How come?*

B: Because nobody would be able to accept jobs in these places if they didn't have their incomes topped up by the state.

A: *What would happen then if* state benefits were cut completely?

B: You'd get an underclass of people who would be forced to turn to crime in order to support themselves and their families. Such a group probably already exists. *There's probably a good argument for* raising benefits.

A: *But surely,* if you raise them too high, people wouldn't bother to work. Once the level of the benefit is higher than their take-home pay, *why should they* do a job?

B: *Precisely, but the answer isn't* to remove benefits from those who really need them. *The solution is* to raise the minimum wage. Then you will increase the incentive to work and the state wouldn't be subsidising businesses which wouldn't otherwise be viable.

A: *You mean* these enterprises couldn't exist were it not for exploitation of the workers.

B: *Well, some of them could* probably survive, but their profits would certainly be lower. *A lot would depend on* the level at which the minimum wage is set.

A: *Of course, there's nothing to prevent* burger bars from moving to other parts of the world where labour is cheaper.

B: *But, who cares if they do? As long as there's* a market for fast food in Britain, someone is going to set up shop. *There may even be* an increase in co-operatives where employees and customers have a share in the profits. *Do we really need* big conglomerates running our economy, when really "small is beautiful"?

17. POLITICAL SYSTEMS

17.4   Questions - discuss in pairs or groups

1.   Would you prefer to live in a society regulated by a democratically elected government or one where levels of income and wealth are mainly regulated by the free market?

2.   Should important utilities such as water, gas and electricity be under government or private ownership? How is it in your country?

3.   Should social services such as schools, hospitals, prisons and social security, be provided mainly from the public purse, or should more be left to the private sector? How is it in your country?

4.   Do Trade Unions serve a useful purpose and should every worker have the right to join one?

5.   Should political power be limited to people who have been democratically elected? Are institutions such as monarchy and The House of Lords now out of date?

6.   Should political parties and politicians have to publish all their sources of income, including private donations?

7.   Should political power be regionalised or centralised?

Dictionary reference

Democracy: a system of government where the people have a say in how government is run.

Autocracy: a system of government where one person has complete power.

The House of Commons: the democratically elected house of the UK parliament responsible for making laws and checking the work of Government.

The House of Lords: the second chamber of the UK parliament, whose members are not elected.

The Prime Minister: the head of an elected government.

The Leader of the Opposition: the leader of the largest political party not in government.

The Cabinet: the committee of senior ministers responsible for controlling government policy

The Shadow Cabinet: committee of senior members of Parliament representing the opposition.

The Chancellor of the Exchequer: the government's chief financial minister and one of the most senior members of the Cabinet.

17. POLITICAL SYSTEMS

The Home Secretary: the senior minister responsible for law and order, police and prisons, and other domestic matters such as nationality, immigration, race relations, extradition and deportation.

17.5   Crossword

17. POLITICAL SYSTEMS

Clues

ACROSS

4. The Socialist Party - traditionally left of centre (6)
7. The part of the economy which is not run by the state (7,6)
9. Identity (2)
10. The minister for overseas affairs (7,9)
11. Enjoyment; a good time (3)
13. Your mother's sister is your _ _ _ _ (4)
14. Place where politicians drink (3)
15. Unwell (3)
19. To do away with (3)
20. The opposite of "west" (4)
21. Extremely dry (4)
22. It has finished. It's _ _ _ _ (4)
23. The house of Commons (7,7)
24. A short letter (4)
26. Master of Arts (2)
27. Layer or level (4)
28. Alcoholic drink liked by sailors (3)
30. To express agreement (6)
32. Usually the role of the second biggest party (10)
34. To move power to the centre (10)
37. Reduction in expenditure (4)
38. Until now (3)
39. Getting older (5)
40. Look after (4)

DOWN

1. Organisation representing the workers (5,5)
2. Ballot to choose the governing party in Britain (7,8)
3. Lorry (5)
4. Centre party in British politics (7,9)
5. A loaf of _ _ _ _ _ (5)
6. The opposite of "beautiful" (4)
8. Parliamentary seats (14)
12. The leader of the ruling party (5,8)
16. Chamber of justice (3,5)
17. The ruling party (10)
18. Paris is in _ _ _ _ _ _ (6)
25. The unelected chamber (3,5)
26. System of government where there is a king or queen (8)
29. The key government ministers (7)
31. Member of Parliament (2)
33. Male monarch (4)
35. A section of a circle (3)
36. The highest in a pack of cards (3)

17. POLITICAL SYSTEMS

Crossword answer key

18. RELIGION

18.1 Find the "odd one out".

[There may be more than one answer. Give your reasons.]

1.	A) Ramadan	B) Lent	C) Christmas
2.	A) an agnostic	B) an atheist	C) a believer
3.	A) free will	B) predetermination	C) fate
4.	A) environmental	B) hereditary	C) innate
5.	A) life after death	B) immortality	C) reincarnation
6.	A) a curate	B) a priest	C) a vicar
7.	A) divinity	B) scripture	C) theology

18.2 Short text (see page 174 for comprehension questions)

A person with a **faith** or **religion** can be referred to as **a believer**. However, in **secular** societies where few people participate in religious **worship**, it is more common to meet **atheists** and **agnostics**. Atheists take the view that there is no **God**. Agnostics simply do not know whether or not God exists. Some may have read many **theological** texts in search of proof one way or the other, though the majority of agnostics probably give little time to questions of religion. This does not necessarily mean that they have no **moral guidelines**. People who have **social consciences** often prefer to describe themselves as **humanists**. They may well share many of the same concerns as **Christians**, **Muslims**, **Hindus**, **Buddhists** or **Jews**. These may relate to war and peace, sexual morality or many other aspects of human relationships.

In Britain, the two largest denominations are **Protestant** and **Catholic**. Both of these groups belong to the Christian church, though the Protestants separated from the Catholic church in the sixteenth century and no longer recognise **the pope** as their head. Among the Protestants are **Anglicans** who are members of the **Church of England**. As you move up through the ranks of **the clergy**, you may start as a **curate**, helping the **vicar** or **rector** in charge of a **parish**. There are several types of **priest**. A successful vicar will move from being a **Reverend** to a **Canon** by which time the **congregation** - the people who attend church - will probably be fairly large. The main administrator of a very large church or cathedral is called the **dean**, though the priest in charge of **the diocese** - a large area such as the city of London or Birmingham - is the **bishop**. The bishop is assisted by an **archdeacon**. The highest ranking bishop - in charge of all the churches in a particular area - is the **archbishop**. The reigning king or queen is the **head** of the Church of England.

18. RELIGION

18.3   Dialogue - read aloud in pairs

A: *Do you believe in* a God who rewards good and punishes wrongdoing?

B: *Well, firstly* I'm an agnostic - I don't know whether or not God exists, but if there is a God I hope he or she doesn't punish wrong-doing.

A: *But why not?* We punish murderers and rapists on Earth, *so why shouldn't* the same people rot in hell?

B: *Because in my view,* I'd prefer to discover an understanding God rather than a God of vengeance. *I'd find it hard to believe in* a God who makes people suffer.

A: But nobody has to suffer. Everybody is free to choose between right and wrong.

B: *Well, that depends on whether* we really have free will. *I happen to believe that* our choices can be traced back to their causes - some hereditary and some environmental.

A: *But if you followed that line to its logical conclusion,* you'd pardon all criminals.

B: *Not at all.* Other people are part of the environment and they have a right to react to wrong-doing to protect society.

A: *Then why shouldn't* God send evil people to hell?

B: *I would agree with you if* the purpose of hell was to rehabilitate people back into heaven, but hell is usually associated with torture and eternal damnation. Civilised countries don't base their prison systems on violent institutions which don't give people a second chance.

A: But God gives people second chances. None of us is perfect, but we have time to confess our sins and to ask for forgiveness.

B: Before the day of judgement, yes, but we can't help what we are and we should be given time to develop even after we have met our creator.

A: *But who can say* that we will develop into civilised beings. *Surely,* God has the right to cut his losses.

B: *I still maintain that* an understanding God would prefer rehabilitation to torture.

18.4   Questions - discuss in pairs or groups

18. RELIGION

1. "The universe is controlled by a God who rewards good and punishes wrongdoing." Do you agree?

2. "True religion is incompatible with war." Do you agree?

3. "There is life after death - for example, heaven, hell or reincarnation." Do you agree?

4. "The story of Adam and Eve is not to be believed. Darwin's theory of evolution is more credible." Do you agree?

5. "It is impossible for the rich to be truly religious. That's why Christians have Lent and Muslims have Ramadan." Do you agree?

6. "It is better to have any religion than to be atheist or agnostic." Do you agree?

7. Do people have *free will* to choose between right or wrong or are our choices determined by hereditary and environmental influences?

8. Are the ten commandments out of date? Which rules do you think are needed for religion or society today?"

9. In Western Europe and the USA, church attendance has gone down. Can you explain why?

10. Should divorced men or women be allowed to re-marry in church?

Dictionary reference

Ramadan: (also spelled Ramadhan or Ramazan) a holy month of worship, study of the Koran (also spelled Quran or Qur'an), prayer and fasting.

Lent: the 40 days before Easter in which some Christians give up something they enjoy.

Atheist: a person who does not believe in the existence of any god or gods.

Agnostic: someone who believes that the existence of God is unknown or unknowable.

Humanist: a person who trusts reason and science and rejects supernatural or divine beliefs.

Free will: having the ability or freedom to choose between different courses of action.

Predetermination: decided beforehand because of character at birth, hereditary and environmental influences.

Hereditary: passing from a parent to a child through the genes.

18. RELIGION

Scripture: the study of the holy writings of a religion, for example the Bible.

Theology: the study of religious belief, practice and experience.

18.5   Crossword

18. RELIGION

ACROSS

1. The highest ranking bishop (10)
9. Crippled (4)
12. The passing on of physical or mental characteristics genetically from one generation to another (8)
15. Something perfect (5)
16. The people who attend church (12)
17. A superhuman being or spirit worshipped as having power over nature (3)
20. Main administrator of a cathedral or very large church (4)
23. A widely accepted principle (5)
25. Believing in or following the religion of Jesus Christ (9)
27. Very uncomfortable (7)
28. Section of a circle (3)
29. Good Christian _ _ _ rejoice and sing! (3)
30. Darwin's theory (9)
33. Myself! (2)
34. Funeral procession (7)
35. Please keep _ _ _ the grass! (3)
36. Asian religion or philosophy teaching the elimination of self and worldly desires (8)
39. Religious laws (12)
42. To confer divine favour upon (5)
44. Condemnation to eternal punishment in hell (9)
47. Someone who doesn't believe or disbelieve (8)
49. Television (2)
51. Nonsense (6)
53. District under the pastoral care of a bishop (7)
55. Bitter grief or distress (3)
56. Noise of a cow (3)
58. Ninth month of the Muslim year during which strict fasting is observed from sunrise to sunset (8)
61. Plural of "is" (3)
63. Your maker (7)
65. An ordained minister of the Roman Catholic, Orthodox or Anglican church (6)
66. Short for "information" (4)
67. Finality (3)
68. The study of theistic religion (8)
69. Belief (5)
70. Belief in a superhuman controlling power (8)

DOWN

1. I think, therefore I _ _ (2)
2. Rebirth of the soul in a new body (13)
3. Hello! (2)
4. Condition (2)
5. Watering place in the desert (5)
6. The place of punishment or torture where the souls of the damned are confined after death (4)
7. Retribution (9)
8. The main religious and social system of India, including belief in reincarnation (8)
10. A bishop's assistant (10)
11. The breaking of divine or moral law (3)
12. Expression of surprise or laughter (2)
13. 40 day period of fasting and penitence (4)
14. The next step up from Reverend (5)
18. A belief or outlook seeking solely rational ways of solving human problems (8)
19. The priest in charge of a large diocese such as a city (6)
21. A member or follower of any of the western Christian churches that are separate from the Roman Catholic Church (10)
22. Roman road - Latin for "through" (3)
24. The day of reckoning (9)
25. A young cow often given as a sacrifice (4)
26. Furnished with a weapon (5)
31. Empty or vacant (4)
32. Jesus _ _ Nazareth (2)
36. Someone who has faith in God (8)
37. Assistance (4)
38. The religion of the Jews (7)
40. _ _ _ _ Dimittis - Now let your servant depart in peace (4)
41. Insane (3)
43. Concerned with the affairs of this world; not spiritual or sacred (7)
45. Someone who doesn't believe in God (7)
46. To admit or confess (4)
48. Capable of being led astray (9)
50. A junior member of the clergy who helps the vicar of a parish (6)
52. A Muslim place of worship (6)
54. General term for curate, vicar or priest (6)
57. An area having its own church and clergy (6)
59. Opposite of "love" (4)
60. Those in need (5)
62. Track or way (4)
64. Surface or space (4)
65. The bishop of Rome as head of the Roman Catholic Church (4)

18. RELIGION

Crossword answer key

19. RICH WORLD : POOR WORLD

19.1 Find the "odd one out".

[There may be more than one answer. Give your reasons.]

1.	A) developed	B) developing	C) underdeveloped
2.	A) to aid	B) to donate	C) to help
3.	A) exploitation	B) oppression	C) colonial occupation
4.	A) an appeal	B) a campaign	C) a good cause
5.	A) charity	B) deprivation	C) need
6.	A) debt	B) drought	C) famine
7.	A) an auxiliary	B) a recruit	C) a volunteer

19.2 Short text (see page 174 for comprehension questions)

The common phrases used to describe **the rich world** include **"the developed countries"** and **"the advanced industrial countries"**. To describe very poor countries, we usually refer to **"the developing countries"** or **"underdeveloped nations"**.

Economists also refer to **"the North South divide"** to emphasise that countries in the **northern hemisphere** are generally richer than those in the **southern hemisphere** - namely Africa and Latin America.

People in the rich world have mixed attitudes towards giving **aid** to poorer countries. Some take the view that **charity** begins at home. It is true that there are many people **in need** in Britain. However, the people who are making the most generous **donations** to domestic charities are often the ones who are supporting emergency **appeals** for the victims of conflicts and disasters overseas. Church-based **campaigns** such as "Christian Aid" and secular ones such as the BBC's "Children in Need" direct themselves to both national and international **causes**.

The **obligation** of the rich world towards the poor world is not based on history alone. As a former **colonial power**, Britain was once responsible for the **slave trade** and the **exploitation** of other countries' **resources**. But today, together with other rich countries, we continue to **dominate** world markets, setting the **terms of trade** in our favour.

19. RICH WORLD : POOR WORLD

19.3   Dialogue - read aloud in pairs

A: What kind of help do you think rich countries should contribute to poorer countries?

B: *Well, there's no doubt that* a proper understanding of their problems is needed before we can go much further.

A: *Surely,* there are immediate things like food aid to countries hit by drought and famine.

B: *Yes, but* you have to be very careful not to kill off local agriculture by dumping great quantities of free food and underpricing their farmers. We really need to give these countries the means to solve their own problems.

A: *How do you do that?*

B: *Well, firstly* we need to take an interest in developing countries instead of just competing with rich countries. *I strongly believe in* preventing problems before they happen. *In much the same way as* the Japanese prepare for earthquakes, countries with dry climates could have water catchment systems and reservoirs to defend against water shortage.

A: *But how do we persuade* the governments of these countries to take these preventative measures rather than spending money on armaments?

B: *Could I suggest that we* stop trying to sell them arms. In the past, we have used many of these countries for our own short-term needs, but we don't have to go on doing so.

A: Then what form of aid *would you recommend?*

B: *I was just coming to that.* There are some very good agencies which recruit volunteers to work on projects in rural communities. They can direct skilled people and material resources to where they are needed. They don't have to get involved with military projects. They can send skilled volunteers into schools and hospitals to train local people to take their places after a number of years.

A: *But, isn't there a danger that* the schools and hospitals will always be staffed by foreigners? When you have successfully trained local people, they usually emigrate to countries where they are paid much higher salaries.

B: *There's always a risk of that.* Projects have to be carefully thought out. You'd naturally try to select trainees with some commitment to their country. *Anyway, it isn't such a bad thing to have* dedicated volunteers working in the field. They can specify what equipment is lacking and this could either be supplied by donor countries or manufactured locally.

19. RICH WORLD : POOR WORLD

19.4   Questions - discuss in pairs or groups

1.   What kind of aid should the governments of rich countries give to poor countries?

2.   "Population control is more important in rich countries than in poor countries since rich babies consume much more of the world's resources than poor ones." Do you agree?

3.   "Economic Unions made up of rich countries are a form of protectionism which prevents fair trade with poor countries." Do you agree?

4.   "Economic colonialism where multinational companies provide most of the work opportunities is just as bad as colonialism where poor countries belong to rich ones." Do you agree?

5.   "It is right for rich countries to have strict immigration controls to stop people from poorer countries entering them and sharing in their better standard of living." Do you agree?

6.   "Immigration should not be limited to people of similar race and culture. We should welcome the opportunity of a truly multi-racial society." Do you agree?

7.   "Everybody should be encouraged to do Voluntary Service Overseas (i.e. to live and work in a developing country) so that we can understand the problems of poorer nations and make a contribution to help them." Do you agree?

8.   Would you like to be an overseas volunteer in a poorer country? If so, which one and how could you contribute to that country's development?

9.   Are *the poor* poor because they are poor or because they are lazy?

Dictionary reference

Developed countries: advanced industrial countries where people generally have high incomes.

Developing countries: countries with little industrial or economic activity where incomes are generally low.

The Third World: a phrase once used to refer to developing countries, now considered to be rather rude and outdated. The charity *Third World First* changed its name to *People & Planet* in 1997.

The North-South Divide: in the context of world economics, this means the difference in wealth between the countries in the northern hemisphere (Europe and North America) and those in the southern hemisphere (Africa, Latin America and much of Asia). In the context of the UK, the same phrase is used to describe the economic, cultural and social differences between Southern and Northern England, London and the South East generally having greater wealth.

19.5 Crossword

19. RICH WORLD : POOR WORLD

Clues

ACROSS

3. Well built; the opposite of slim (3)
6. Attempt to draw public attention to a problem (8)
9. Short for Christine (4)
10. Flying saucer (3)
12. Colour of the communist flag (3)
13. Opposite of free trade (13)
14. Sick (3)
15. Uncommon (4)
16. Help (3)
17. Poor but improving (10)
18. Advanced (9)
20. Rodent with sharp teeth (3)
23. Excluding (6)
25. Pessimism (5)
26. In the past (3)
27. To come out on top (3)
29. Having an appetite through lack of food (6)
30. Unpaid recruit (9)
31. Give (6)
33. Basic cause (4)
35. Money owed (4)
36. Goal (3)
38. Lack of water (7)
39. Request for the public to help (6)

DOWN

1. Pen (4)
2. Backward (14)
3. Absence of food (6)
4. Rules governing transactions (5,2,5)
5. Support worker (9)
6. A good cause (7)
7. Made of pulp (5)
8. Obtain (3)
9. Poor nations (5,5)
11. Duty (10)
16. Combine (3)
19. Rule as master (8)
21. Use unfairly for profit or gain (7)
22. Materials (9)
24. Open-topped pie (4)
28. To buy from other countries (6)
31. Gap (6)
32. Deprivation (4)
33. Entitlements (6)
34. Reside (4)
37. Plan (3)

19. RICH WORLD : POOR WORLD

Crossword answer key

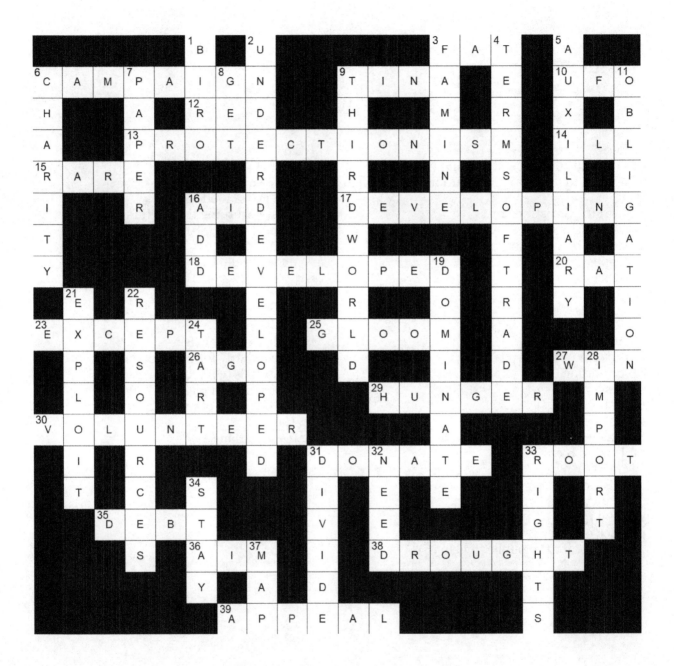

20. SCIENCE & TECHNOLOGY

20.1 Find the "odd one out".

[There may be more than one answer. Give your reasons.]

1.	A) Biology	B) Chemistry	C) Natural Science
2.	A) a subject	B) a discipline	C) a topic
3.	A) computing	B) Information Technology	C) Artificial Intelligence
4.	A) USB flash drive	B) Hard drive	C) SD memory card
5.	A) sources	B) references	C) resources
6.	A) to investigate	B) to research	C) to study
7.	A) to analyse	B) to evaluate	C) to test
8.	A) accessible	B) simple	C) user-friendly

20.2 Short text (see page 174 for comprehension questions)

British parents may find it difficult to help their children with their Science and Technology homework. as the teaching of these disciplines has changed radically.

Science is no longer presented as **Physics**, **Chemistry** and **Biology** to be learnt parrot fashion, but as a **practical discipline** requiring **communication skills** and the application of **knowledge** and **understanding**. Pupils now have to behave like scientists in and outside the classroom. They learn to **communicate**, whether working alone or contributing to a **group effort**. They learn **research skills** such as the use of **reference materials**. They practise **gathering** and **organising** information from different **sources**. They develop the ability to **record** and **report** as well as to **translate** information from one form to another to **suit** a particular audience or purpose. **Familiarity** with computers is now essential as pupils are expected to use **spreadsheets** and **databases** as well as **presentation software** .

Technology was previously encountered as an **option** at Secondary School and often limited to **Technical Drawing.** It is now **compulsory** for pupils aged between five and sixteen. As in Science, the **new approach** is based on **practice**. Pupils are encouraged to identify opportunities for **design** and technological activities and to express them verbally. They learn these abilities in the **contexts** of home, school, recreation, community and also **business** and **industry** as they approach school-leaving age. They also learn to **generate** designs, to **plan** and make things using **appropriate resources** and to **evaluate** the processes, products and effects of their design and

20. SCIENCE & TECHNOLOGY

technological activities. **Computer literacy** from an early age and the ability to use **Artificial Intelligence** systems and **computer-aided design** programs now form important parts of the Technology syllabus.

20.3   Dialogue - read aloud in pairs

A: *Do you think* that it is possible to get computers to think, learn and act like humans?

B: *That's an interesting question, because* artificial intelligence systems are improving all the time.

A: *How do you mean?*

B: *Well*, machines are being trained using algorithms and vast amounts of data to recognise patterns, make predictions, learn from experience and adapt to new situations in a similar way to what humans do.

A: What are algorithms?

B: *I can answer that.* They are simply a set of commands which must be followed by a computer to perform calculations or other problem-solving operations.

A: *Would you like to* give me some examples?

B: *Well*, getting breakfast, following a recipe or trying on a new pair of trousers all involve step by step routines which need to be completed in a specific order.

A: *Then* why are automated systems so bad? *I mean* when I include a French word in a text message on my smart phone, the system usually changes it to an English word that is quite different from my intended meaning.

B: *Yes,* that can be very irritating. The system is too basic to recognise that you communicate using two languages, but systems can learn given the right data. A more advanced system would probably be used in voice recognition software. You would be able to train it to recognise your pronunciation. A good system could be trained to accommodate a regional accent.

A: Can you give me some examples of uses of artificial intelligence in everyday life ?

B: *Firstly,* there are personal assistants like Siri, Google Assistant and Amazon Alexa. These all use AI algorithms to perform tasks, answer questions and make personalised recommendations. *Then* there is Google Maps , an AI-driven navigation app which uses real-time traffic data. *A third example is* social media sites. Here AI algorithms are widely used to personalise content based on your likes and interests.

20. SCIENCE & TECHNOLOGY

A: Are there any more serious applications?

B: *Yes, certainly.* AI systems are increasingly used in healthcare improving diagnostic accuracy and efficiency, for example by assisting radiologists in interpreting medical images like X-rays, MRIs, and CT scans. Algorithms are also used in language translation of both text and speech. The examples of what they can do are endless.

20.4   Questions - discuss in pairs or groups

1.   What do you think are the main dangers of scientific advances? What laws do you think we need to protect societies from these dangers?

2.   Do you think Science will (a) end the world (b) save the world or (c) do neither?

3.   Have computers and smart phones changed society for the better or for the worse?

3.   Do you make use of artificial intelligence systems in your every day life? If so, which applications?

4.   At what age should Science and Technology start to be taught? Describe your school experience of these subjects. Did you have to choose between Arts or Science subjects?

5.   Do you prefer phone helplines where you are answered by human beings rather than automated systems? Describe any occasion where an automated response has left you feeling frustrated.

Dictionary reference

Natural science: this subject includes life science known as biology, and physical science which includes the branches of physics, chemistry, earth science and astronomy.

Artificial intelligence: technology which enables computers and machines to simulate human intelligence and problem-solving capabilities.

Algorithms: sets of commands which a computer must follow step by step to perform calculations or other problem-solving operations.

CAD/CAM: computer assisted design and manufacture.

Reference materials: various sources that provide background information or quick facts on any given topic.

Resources: a supply of materials (which can include things, staff, or money).

20. SCIENCE & TECHNOLOGY

20.5   Crossword

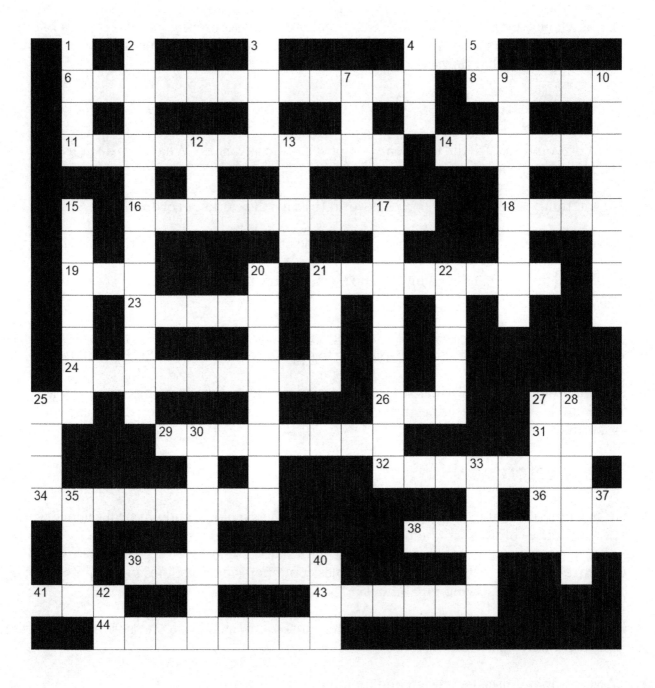

Clues

ACROSS

4. Large wall across a stretch of water (3)
6. Easy to operate or understand (4-8)
8. Preposition (5)
11. Program allowing manipulation and retrieval of tabulated numerical data (11)
14. Choice (6)
16. Obligatory (10)
18. Back (4)
19. Purchase (3)
21. Special study (8)
23. Firing of guns at the same time (5)
24. Study of the elements (9)
25. Information Technology (2)
26. Computer Assisted Design (3)
27. Compact Disk (2)
29. Structured set of data held in a computer (8)
31. The colour of British pillar boxes (3)
32. References (7)
34. The mechanical and electronic components of a computer (8)
36. Not bright (3)
38. Nature Study (7)
39. Study of the properties of matter and energy (7)
41. Alternative to coffee (3)
43. Spies (6)
44. Knowing how to add up, subtract, multiply and divide (8)

DOWN

1. Divides (4)
2. Measuring in tens (6, 6)
3. Children (4)
4. Colouring (3)
5. Master of Arts (2)
7. Expected soon (3)
9. Knowing how to read (8)
10. Make (8)
12. Running between hand and shoulder (3)
13. Incline (4)
15. Topic (7)
17. Materials (9)
20. Programs used by a computer (8)
21. Red jewel (4)
22. Combined (5)
25. Just over two centimetres (4)
27. Latin for "I believe".
28. Plan (6)
30. Examine in detail (7)
33. Origins (5)
35. A large area of land (4)
37. Possessive Adjective for 1st Person singular (2)
40. Pronounce (3)
42. Indefinite article before a vowel (2)

20. SCIENCE & TECHNOLOGY

Crossword answer key

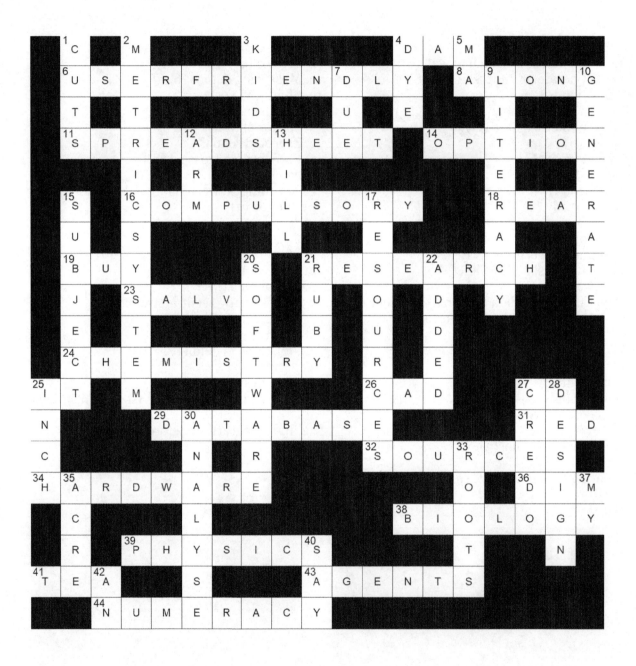

21. SOCIETY

21.1   Find the "odd one out".

[There may be more than one answer. Give your reasons.]

1.   A) a community   B) a neighbourhood   C) a locality

2.   A) a civilian   B) a citizen   C) a soldier

3.   A) euthanasia   B) suicide   C) murder

4.   A) a vision   B) a dream   C) a hope

5.   A) classless   B) democratic   C) egalitarian

6.   A) the age of consent   B) the age of majority   C) the age of reason

7.   A) a consensus   B) a census   C) a general agreement

21.2   Short text (see page 175 for comprehension questions)

The meaning of **"society"** is susceptible to changes in place and time. In Britain, during the Second World War, there was a feeling of **community** because **civilians** helped one another out. When the war ended, the **Welfare State** was founded. People were provided with **free eye tests, glasses, medicines** and **dental check-ups**. There was a sense of the strong helping the weak. By the end of the 1950s, many people were purchasing washing machines and televisions. Some were even buying their own houses. The **consumer society** was under way. Politicians told us that we'd never had it so good.

During the 1960s, in both Britain and America, the **conventional view** of society was challenged by a **youth movement** whose opinions were articulated through **pop** and **folk music** and **student politics**. Songs such as **"Little Boxes"** ridiculed the idealised picture of the **two parent family** whose children went through both summer school and university to become **perfect products** of society. The little boxes of many different colours which all looked just the same, were the suburban dwellings of the American middle class. Other songs such as **"What did you learn in school, today?"** questioned the image of the **good citizen** who never doubts the teacher's word, regards the police as friends, supports the death penalty and is eager to fight for his country. The attack on the **uniformity of the family** developed into a **protest against the Vietnam war**. By the early 1970s, criticism turned to the **corruption** inherent in **the Nixon administration**.

Today, people show greater tolerance towards different family structures such as **single parent families** and there is a wider acceptance of **different races** and **sexualities**. However, trust is in short supply, judging by the number of **dash cams** fitted in cars and **CCTV cameras** used outside homes. The number of people who work from home has increased because they now have the technology to do so. Moreover, **Covid 19** resulted in a permanent change in many people's **working habits**.

21.3   Dialogue - read aloud in pairs

A: Many politicians have visions of a better society. *Do you have such a vision?*

B: *I'll need time to think about that.* If you can describe the visions of the different political parties, *then I'll tell you where I stand.*

A: *O.K. I'll start with* the Labour Party. *It seems that* they want gradual change towards a more equitable society with improvements to education, health and public transport. The Conservatives seem to favour free market principles and individual responsibility. They prioritise law and order and take a tough stance on crime and immigration. The Liberal Democrats take a centrist approach. They support membership of international organisations such as the EU, they prioritise civil liberties and human rights, and being the smallest party, they are eager to change the voting system.

B: *Don't you think* the vision of the three major parties is more or less the same?

A: Well, it has to be to some extent. They're out for votes. They've learnt that people are wise to promises which can't be delivered; in fact, they probably don't want too much upheaval in their lives.

B: Do any of the minor parties offer promises of greater change?

A: *I think we can forget about* the far right parties, because *there now seems to be a general acceptance* that Britain is a multi-racial society as well as a fairly tight stance on immigration. The Green Party is of far greater interest, because their vision relates to everything we produce and consume and the effects of all our actions on the environment. The effects of global warming on the climate are increasingly gaining publicity.

B: *But surely,* the Greens will never get enough support to win a General Election.

A: *No, but you can be certain that* the major political parties will steal their clothes. Everybody notices when town centres become clogged up with cars, when the air in their streets becomes polluted, when it becomes dangerous to swim in the sea and when water tastes of pesticides.

B: *You mean it's possible to* ignore the Green Party, but you can't ignore their policies when a general consensus of people come to support them?

A: *Exactly.*

21. SOCIETY

B: *Well, I think I'll go along with* the Green Party's vision of society, *but I'm not sure that* I'll vote for them. You see, I want my vote to count.

A: You should vote for what you believe in. Then there's far more chance that the major parties *will sit up and take notice.*

21.4   Questions - discuss in pairs or groups

1.   How is the society you live in different today from what it was ten or twenty years ago?

2.   What are the visions of society belonging to the main political parties in your country? Are they very different?

3.   At what ages do you think people should be allowed to (a) leave school (b) leave home (c) buy alcoholic drinks (d) join the armed forces (e) start a family (f) vote in General Elections?

4.   Do you believe in a high tax economy as in Scandinavian countries where services such as state education and health are well funded, or a low tax economy as in the USA where people make private provision for good services?

5.   Are the police in your country able to (a) carry guns (b) stop and search people in the street?

6.   Which is more important - to be tough on crime or to be tough on the causes of crime?

7.   Should euthanasia (assisted dying) be legally available to people in great pain who want to die?

8   Do you have a vision of a better society? What changes would you make?

9.   What do you think are the characteristics of a good member of society? Are there things that parents and schools can do to create good citizens?

Dictionary reference

The nanny state: a term used to describe a government which is overprotective or which interferes unduly with freedom of choice.

Devil take the hindmost: letting people do what's best for themselves without thinking of other people. Putting oneself first and leaving others behind.

Census: population survey.

21. SOCIETY

21.5   Crossword

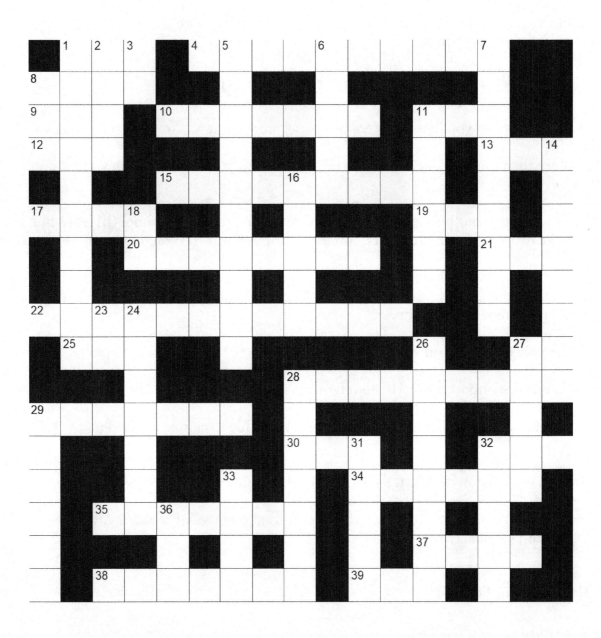

21. SOCIETY

Clues

ACROSS
1. Automobile (3)
4. Decided by the people (10)
8. Come together (4)
9. Weapon (3)
10. Civilian (7)
11. Car with no windows (3)
12. A married lady (3)
13. A watering place (3)
15. Egalitarian (9)
17. Not shut (4)
19. Hotel (3)
20. Neighbourhood (8)
21. A gentleman (3)
22. Call up for military service (12)
25. National Farmers' Union (3)
27. Calling attention to an amazing sight (2)
28. Learning (9)
29. Regular meeting with dentist (5-2)
30. A time in history (3)
32. Plead (3)
34. Unlawful killing (6)
35. Health (7)
37. A nomad's home (4)
38. The age when it is lawful to have sex (7)
39. Homosexual (3)

DOWN
1. Wrongdoing (10)
2. Objectives (4)
3. Royal Navy (2)
5. Mercy killing (10)
6. Large fishing basket (5)
7. General agreement (9)
8. Preserves (3)
11. Dream (6)
14. Termination of a pregnancy (8)
16. St (5)
18. Dutch (2)
23. National Front (2)
24. Taking your own life (7)
26. The age when you are allowed to vote (8)
27. Not a winner (5)
28. Meeting with optician (3-4)
29. Population survey (6)
31. Preposition - in the midst (5)
32. Creature (5)
33. Ethnic origin (4)
36. Local Area Network (3)

21. SOCIETY

Crossword answer key

	1 C	2 A	3 R		4 D	5 E	M	O	6 C	R	A	T	I	7 C	
8 J	O	I	N			U			R					O	
9 A	R	M		10 C	I	T	I	Z	E	N		11 V	A	N	
12 M	R	S				H		E		I		13 S	P	14 A
	U		15 C	L	A	16 S	S	L	E	S	S	E		B
17 O	P	E	18 N		N		A		19 I	N	N		O
	T		20 L	O	C	A	L	I	T	Y		O	21 S	I	R	T
	I			S		N		N		U	I
22 C	O	23 N	24 S	C	R	I	P	T	I	O	N	S	I
	25 N	F	U		A			26 M	27 L	O
		I		28 E	D	U	C	A	T	I	O	N
29 C	H	E	C	K	U	P	Y	J	S
E			30 E	R	31 A	O	32 B	E	G
N	D	33 R	T	34 M	U	R	D	E	R
S	35 W	E	36 L	F	A	R	E	O	I	I
U	A	C	S	N	37 T	E	N	T
S	38 C	O	N	S	E	N	T	39 G	A	Y	G

22. SPORT

22.1   Find the "odd one out".

[There may be more than one answer. Give your reasons.]

1.	A) a game	B) a sport	C) a match
2.	A) betting	B) gambling	C) gaming
3.	A) a competition	B) a contest	C) an event
4.	A) the Test Match	B) the FA Cup Final	C) the World Cup
5.	A) a crew	B) a side	C) a team
6.	A) to lose a game	B) to miss a game	C) to win a game
7.	A) football	B) rugby	C) soccer
8.	A) judge	B) referee	C) umpire

22.2   Short text (see page 175 for comprehension questions)

There are several different categories of sports which exercise both the body and mind.

Altitude sports include **gliding, hang-gliding, mountaineering** and **parachuting**. They are not for people who are afraid of heights.

Athletics includes **track and field** events involving **running, jumping, vaulting** and **throwing**. A standard track is a circuit of 400 metres. The field is the green area in the middle.

Combat games consist of **boxing, fencing, judo, karate, kendo** and **wrestling**.

Court games attract people of all ages. They include **badminton, basketball, handball, netball, pelota, squash, table tennis, tennis** and **volleyball**. The courts are **rectangular.**

Equestrian sports, usually for people rich enough to own horses, include **dressage, eventing, horse racing, polo** and **show jumping**. Many people enjoy **betting** on the horses.

Field sports require a large **area of green**. They include **American football, baseball, bowls, cricket, croquet. golf, hockey, lacrosse, rugby football** and **soccer**.

127

22. SPORT

Gymnasium sports consist of **weightlifting** and **gymnastics**. The latter contains **floor exercises** including **leaps, spins, balances** and **tumbles** as well as **fixed apparatus** such as **rings, bars, beams, pommel horses** and **vaulting horses**.

Other categories of sport are (1) **target** (2) **water** (3) **wheeled** and (4) **winter sports**. Can you think of some examples of these categories?

22.3   Dialogue - read aloud in pairs

A: *Do you think it's possible* to keep politics out of sport?

B: Not at national or international level.

A: *Why not?*

B: Well, we can hardly keep politics out of the Eurovision song contest. *How are we meant to* keep it out of football, which has a far greater following?

A: *I'd certainly agree if you're thinking of* the World Cup. Success in such a major tournament seems to produce a feel-good factor which benefits ruling political parties. Failure produces the opposite effect.

B: *Also,* the very act of hosting the World Cup or the Olympics gives a great boost to tourism because of all the spectators who come to watch their country and the opportunities to present favourable images to the media.

A: *Yet, there are surely some features* of these events which are above politics. *What about* the power of the athletes and the artistic beauty of the synchronised swimmers?

B: *But why* play the gold medalists' national anthems and why carry flags?

A: *I think you're being too sceptical.* Sporting greats such as Pelé and Mohamed Ali are remembered for their skill, not for their nationality.

B: Of course, in Ali's case he is indeed remembered for his politics too. He put a little known African country on the map, highlighted the causes of draft-dodgers and black Muslims and rescued hostages. What could be more political than that?

A: He was certainly political, yet he succeeded in endearing himself to millions of whites and raised the moral of millions of blacks. *You may be right about* sport and politics, but there can be positive outcomes which go beyond excessive nationalism.

22. SPORT

22.4 Questions - discuss in pairs or groups

1. Which is more important in sport - winning or taking part? Are you a good loser?

2. Should we always try to keep politics out of sport?

3. In Britain, the big sporting events include the Boat Race, the Grand National & the Derby (horse races), the World Snooker Championship, the Six Nations (rugby), the FA Cup Final (football), Wimbledon (tennis), the British Grand Prix (formula 1 motor racing) and the Test Match (cricket). Which of these would you most like to see? Why?

4. What are the most important events in the sporting calendar in your country? Which of these events do you enjoy watching most? Why?

5. Is it easy to take part in sport in your country? Which sports do you do? How often do you take part? How good are you at them?

6. Who are your sporting heroes and heroines? Why do you admire them?

7. Should the Olympic Games be held only in Greece or should they change between different countries? Where would you like to see them held next time?

8. Should boxing and other combat sports be included in the school curriculum?

9. Which is your favourite sport to watch and what do you think are the qualities of a good team or a true champion in that sport?

10. How would you encourage people who sit around at home all the time to do more sport?

Dictionary reference

The World Cup: the highest level football tournament held once every four years.

The Olympic Games: a series of international sporting competitions held in a different country during the summer and the winter once every four years.

The Test Match: one of a series of cricket matches played by the national representatives of two countries. The term is also used to describe rugby matches between nations.

The Eurovision Song Contest: an annual singing competition broadcast on live television involving European countries which are members of the European Broadcasting Union.

22. SPORT

22.5 Crossword

22. SPORT

Clues

ACROSS

5. Racing in a boat with a mast (7)
8. Riding on a plank of wood on wheels (13)
9. Anger (4)
11. Website address (3)
13. Occupation (3)
14. Played with hands, a ball and a high net (10)
16. Place oneself on a chair (3)
17. Become tired (4)
18. A long, thin, snake-like fish (3)
19. Look after (4)
20. Racing in a pool (8)
22. Supporter (3)
24. Opposite of "yes" (2)
25. A heavy weight (3)
27. Played with ten pins (7)
29. _ _ Went Gone (2)
30. You need a long line and a river or lake (7)
32. Flying for human beings with large kites (4-7)
35. Putting money on the outcome of races or games (7)
37. Governor (4)
40. In good health (3)
42. Played by the globetrotters (10)
45. Primary colour (3)
46. Do Did _ _ _ _ (4)
47. Played with rackets and a shuttlecock (9)
48. Riding on two planks of wood on snow (6)
51. Running, hurdling and other exercises (9)
53. Martial art done with hands and feet (6)
54. Racing in a boat with oars (6)
55. Fashion (5)

DOWN

1. Ping pong (5,6)
2. A form of body building (13)
3. Done by jockeys (5,6)
4. To score a victory (3)
6. Keep fit exercises often done to music (8)
7. Long country walks (8)
8. A racket game played within the walls of a small room (6)
10. Played with clubs on large greens (4)
12. Equestrian sport (5,6)
13. Half walking and half running (7)
15. To be beaten by the other side (4)
21. Type of food made from unleavened dough (7)
22. 5th (5)
23. Soccer (8)
26. Opposite of "off" (2)
28. Ultimate (4)
31. Played with an oval ball and two sets of posts (5)
33. Against (4)
34. Making artistic shapes on a cold surface (3,7)
36. Racket game played on grass or a hard court (6)
38. Unhappy (3)
39. A side (4)
41. 10th (5)
43. A group of musicians (4)
44. A bat and ball game played in England and Australia (7)
45. Area for ice skating (4)
46. To come equal with the other side (4)
49. Used for rowing (4)
50. Repair (4)
52. Not high (3)

22. SPORT

Crossword answer key

23. TRADITIONS

23.1 Find the "odd one out".

[There may be more than one answer. Give your reasons.]

1.   A) a legend   B) a myth   C) a tradition

2.   A) Robin Hood   B) The Loch Ness   C) William Tell
                              Monster

3.   A) a celebration   B) a ceremony   C) a custom

4.   A) May day   B) April Fool's day   C) St Valentine's day

5.   A) Hogmanay   B) Halloween   C) New Year's day

6.   A) a feast   B) a festivity   C) a festival

7.   A) contemporary   B) popular   C) traditional

8.   A) to review   B) to revise   C) to revive

23.2 Short text (see page 175 for comprehension questions)

In a world of technological change, we struggle to keep up with new developments, yet at the same time, many of us welcome the **continuity** and **repetition** provided by **traditions**. Some of our traditions are connected with places; others relate to the **calendar** and **religious** or **pagan ceremonies.**

There are a number of towns and cities in Britain which are associated with **legendary people** or **creatures**. Tourists visiting Nottingham can take a trip to **Sherwood forest** where they can revive the legend of **Robin Hood**. A journey to **Loch Ness**, near Inverness in Scotland, may result in a sighting of **"Nessie"** the famous **monster.** London is rich in traditions such as the **changing of the guards at Buckingham Palace** and **Horse Guards Parade**. The **opening of parliament** when members of the **House of Commons** are called to the **House of Lords** to attend the **King's Speech** is just one of many annual events.

Annual religious ceremonies provide us with **holly, fir trees** and **crackers** at **Christmas,** and **chocolate eggs** at **Easter**. Other yearly events include **Burns' Night** in January to celebrate the birth of Scotland's great national poet, **pancake day** in February, **April Fools' Day** on 1st April, **the crowning of the May Queen** on 1st May and **bonfire night** on 5th November. Traditions are also observed during important moments of our lives such as **weddings** and **funerals.**

23. TRADITIONS

In a traditional British church wedding, the **bride** wears a **long white dress** while the **groom** wears a **black cloak** and **top hat**. The **bride's father** escorts her to the front of the church and she is attended by **brides maids** when she leaves. The groom, accompanied by the **"best man"** brings a **gold ring** which is placed on the bride's finger after the couple have made serious promises. The groom is then allowed to kiss the bride.

23.3 Dialogue - read aloud in pairs

A: *Do you think we should* maintain our traditions or make way for change?

B: In country's like Japan, people have done both, though it's usually older people who pass on the traditions. The young are often embarrassed by them. This is a shame.

A: *Why do you say that?*

B: *Let me explain. Take* a traditional Japanese song, *for example. Perhaps* children are taught to sing this song by their grandmother when they are five years old. *Well,* when they reach the age of fifteen, they reject the songs of their childhood. *Instead,* they are into pop or rock songs which will be forgotten within weeks.

A: *But, that's quite natural.* Teenagers have always had an appetite for fast food.

B: *It would be O.K. if* they recognised the quality of the songs that their grandmother had taught them and went on to sing them to their own grandchildren.

A: *Why shouldn't they? After all,* these songs have been handed down for generations. If they're any good, *then surely* they'll survive.

B: *I'm not so sure about that.*

A: *Why not?*

B: *Because* traditions are now under attack from mass production and mass marketing.

A: *What do you mean?*

B: Music today is owned by large multinational recording companies usually located in developed countries. The same applies to soft drinks.

A: *I don't understand. What's the connection between* a folk song and a soft drink?

23. TRADITIONS

B: *Well, take* the Spanish drink "horchata". This is a very nice, traditional, vegetable based drink for people who don't want to drink alcohol. *However, try to* order it in a number of Spanish bars *and you'll find that* it has almost become extinct.

A: *Come on!* I bet that you can get traditional Spanish wines and beers!

B: *That isn't the point. I'm talking about* soft drinks and few Spanish bars will serve you with "horchata", their own traditional soft drink. *However,* they'll be delighted to serve you with commercial soft drinks which will be advertised all over the walls of the bar and on the signs outside. *It's the same with* music. The oral traditions of small countries are being submerged by inferior imports.

23.4   Questions - discuss in pairs or groups

1. Do children in your country learn traditional songs which their grandparents also know? What are these songs about? Do children become ashamed of them as they become teenagers?

2. Does your country have any traditional dances to accompany special ceremonies at different times of the year? Describe the dances and the traditional dance costumes.

3. Traditional food in Britain includes roast beef and Yorkshire pudding, fish & chips and haggis while traditional drinks include beer (best bitter) and whisky. What traditional food and drinks do you have in your country?

4. In Britain, when you are invited to a dinner party, it is traditional to bring a bottle of wine and flowers or chocolates for the hostess. It is normal to arrive on time, but not too early. What happens in your country?

5. London businessmen used to wear grey suits and bowler hats. They also carried umbrellas and read The Times newspaper. What is the traditional image of business people in your capital city?

6. In very traditional British schools, the pupils stand up when the teacher enters the room. Teachers used to wear square black hats and long black gowns. It is also traditional to have school assemblies before morning lessons and to sing a special school song at the end of term. Do schools in your country have similar traditions?

7. In the British calendar, the traditional ceremonies include Hogmanay (the Scottish New Year), pancake day in February, dancing on 1st May and bonfire night in November when we burn an effigy of the man who tried to blow up Parliament. When are the traditional ceremonies in your country and what happens?

8. Describe a traditional wedding ceremony in your country.

9. Describe the traditions relating to your country's Royal Family, Centre of Government, General Elections or System of Justice.

23.5 Crossword

23. TRADITIONS

Clues

ACROSS
1. Famous resident of Sherwood Forest (5,4)
5. An unbroken succession (10)
8. Car with no doors (3)
9. A day or period of celebration, religious or secular (8)
11. A Scottish monster (4,4)
12. Armed hostilities between nations (3)
13. Small sheep (4)
16. Following modern ideas or fashion in style or design (12)
17. The bringing back of a former custom or practice (7)
18. Cloth (3)
19. The annual ceremony of Christ's birth (9)
23. Belonging to him (3)
24. Cravate (3)
25. Past tense of "meet" (3)
26. Shrove Tuesday (7,3)
28. The burial or cremation of a dead person with its ceremonies (7)
31. Wages or salary (3)
33. Opposite of west (4)
34. An annual religious celebration or an annual village festival (5)
35. A particular established way of behaving or acting (6)
37. Of or carried on by the general public (7)
38. A marriage ceremony (7)

DOWN
1. A general survey or assessment of a subject or thing (6)
2. 5th November (7,5)
3. Landlord of an inn (4)
4. Ancient stringed instruments (5)
5. An event marked with festivities (11)
6. Where the king or queen sits (6)
7. Opposite of day (5)
10. A festive celebration (9)
13. Part of the mouth (3)
14. A re-examination and improvement, especially of a written or printed matter (8)
15. The festival commemorating Christ's resurrection (6)
16. A formal religious or public occasion especially celebrating a particular event (8)
17. Royal Society of Arts (3)
20. Walk on one leg (3)
21. A custom, opinion, or belief handed down to posterity especially orally or by practice (9)
22. Unhappy (3)
27. A traditional story usually involving supernatural or imaginary persons (4)
29. The ninth month of the Muslim year during which strict fasting is observed from sunrise to sunset (7)
30. A traditional story sometimes popularly regarded as historical (6)
31. Irreligious; worshipping nature (5)
32. Like (2)
34. Sparing or economical (6)
36. Stitch (3)

Crossword answer key

23. TRADITIONS

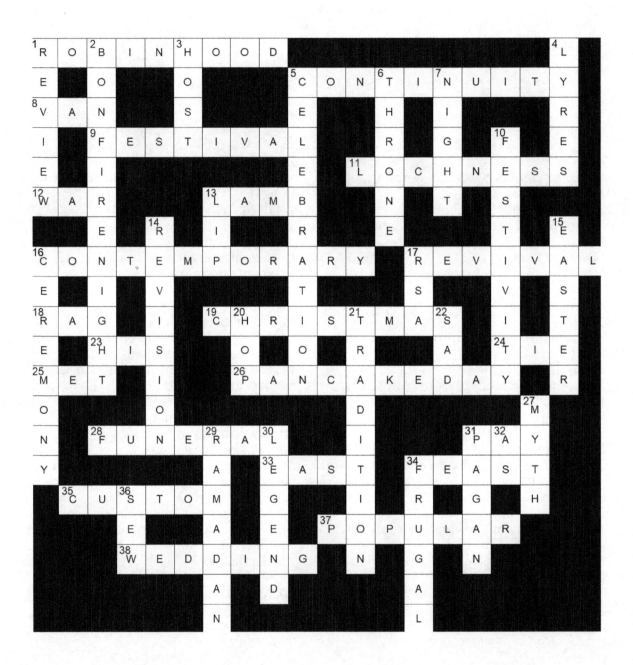

24. TRANSPORT

24.1 Find the "odd one out".

[There may be more than one answer. Give your reasons.]

1.	A) transport	B) travel	C) tourism
2.	A) a byway	B) a highway	C) a main road
3.	A) a footpath	B) a pavement	C) a sidewalk
4.	A) cargo	B) freight	C) luggage
5.	A) the boot	B) the cabin	C) the trunk
6.	A) the accelerator	B) the clutch	C) the throttle
7.	A) a lorry	B) a truck	C) a van
8.	A) a corner	B) a street	C) a turning

24.2 Short text (see page 176 for comprehension questions)

The following description may be useful for **learner drivers** who are also learning English.

When you get into a car for the first time, it is often necessary to **adjust the position** of both the **driver's seat** and the **driving mirror**. The two **wing mirrors** may also need adjusting. Don't forget to **fasten** your **seat belt**. Before **turning the ignition** to **start the engine**, it is wise to check that the **gear** is in **neutral.** The **hand brake** will probably be on.

Once the engine is started, you should look over your right shoulder. You can then **depress the clutch** - the **foot pedal** on the left, **change into first gear**, release the hand brake, **let out the clutch gently** while **depressing the accelerator** very slightly. If you let out the clutch too quickly, the engine will **stall**. As soon as the car is moving, you should depress the clutch again before **changing up into second gear**. The clutch is then released and the same routine is repeated for changing up into higher gears, down into lower ones or into **reverse.**

Good drivers always hold the **steering wheel** with both hands when possible. If they plan to **turn left** or **right,** they **indicate** or **signal** in good time. The **electronic indicator** is usually just to the right of the steering wheel on **right hand drive** cars. The **rod** to the left of the steering wheel usually operates the **windscreen wipers** which you will need if it starts to rain.

Other controls are mounted on the **dashboard**, the smart panel in front of you. You will usually find the switches for the **sidelights** and **headlights**. The electronic indicator is pulled in or pushed out to set the headlights to **dipped** or **full beam**. The **horn** can either be found in the centre of the **steering column** or on one of adjoining rods. Happy **motoring**!

24.3   Dialogue - read aloud in pairs

A: *I believe you've been* working on a transport policy for Britain. Can you explain what is special about your plan?

B: *Yes, certainly. First of all*, Britain is unique in its transport history.

A: *Why's that?*

B: *Because of* the number of different the transport systems that have been developed over the last 300 years. By the year 1700, Britain had a whole network of canals and rivers. Coal could be moved from Welsh mining villages right into the heart of London.

A: *But surely*, the canal system is much too slow for industry today.

B: *Not necessarily. With a bit of forward planning*, we could still move construction materials by waterway, *though I'd agree* that the main potential of canal routes today is their recreational use. *They are ideal for* people who really want to relax and live life at a slower pace - *I don't mean* stuck on the roads in a traffic jam.

A: *What do you propose for* industry then?

B: *Well*, Britain's rail network is still second to none.

A: *But* freight trains can't deliver goods from door to door. *By the time you've* loaded them onto a truck, you might as well do the whole journey by road.

B: *That doesn't necessarily follow.* A lot of our trade is with Europe and before the Channel Tunnel, there was a very good container industry. The containers could either be hooked onto lorries or loaded onto ships. *Why not* adapt the rail network to allow it to cope with containers?

A: *You couldn't have* loading bays and cranes at every station along the line.

B: *No, but you could have* freight terminals in each of our major cities. Loading could take place during the night to avoid congestion.

A: *How do people fit into your plan?*

24. TRANSPORT

B: *Well firstly, nobody will have the right to* own a private car. *You will still be able to* rent a car for journeys between cities, but it will always be cheaper to take the family on the train. There will be taxis to cross town, but it will naturally be more economical to use bicycles and buses or to walk. Disabled people will be given taxi vouchers and there will still be hospital cars driven by professionals.

24.4   Questions - discuss in pairs or groups

1.   Which is your favourite means of private transport?

2.   Do you drive a car? When did you learn to drive? What make of car do you drive? What skills do you need to practise to pass the driving test in your country? Did you pass your test first time? What do you find most difficult about driving?

3.   Which is your favourite form of public transport? Do you prefer (a) buses or trains? (b) ships or planes?

4.   How do you usually travel to work or college in your country?

5   Are you in favour of more road building to create more space for the private motorist in your country?

6.   Do you think that more cycle lanes are needed in your own town or city? What would be some of the problems in providing more facilities for cyclists?

7 .   Do you think that more freight should be sent by rail? Why are companies reluctant to send their goods this way? What needs to be done to change their minds?

8.   Do you think your government should facilitate or discourage private jet travel?

9.   What transport policies are needed to address the challenge of global warming? What kind of vehicles do you think we'll be using in 50 years time?

Dictionary reference

American English: highway, sidewalk, trunk, throttle, truck.

British English: main road, pavement, boot, accelerator, lorry.

24. TRANSPORT

24.5 Crossword

24. TRANSPORT

Clues

ACROSS
1. Americans call it the trunk (4)
3. Type of orange (5)
6. Pedal depressed when changing gear (6)
9. The A23 for example (4,4)
10. Travel for pleasure and the industry which supports such activity (7)
12. Selfish (4)
14. 3rd person singular of the verb TO BE (2)
15. Americans call it the sidewalk (8)
16. SOS (4)
17. Japanese food made of mashed soya beans (4)
19. Japanese woman married to John Lennon (3)
20. Street (2)
22. Speed (4)
23. Expressing the sound of a hiccup (3)
25. Backwards (7)
27. Direction (3)
28. Calf meat (4)
31. Dismissed (5)
33. Hooter (4)
34. 365 days (4)
36. Indicate (6)
39. Wander (4)
43. Local law (5)
44. Travellers carry it (7)
45. Used to pull sledges in the Arctic (4)
47. To pull (3)
48. Street or junction (7)

DOWN
1. Strong ray of light (4)
2. Vehicles which move and carry things and people (9)
3. Corner (8)
4. Route for ramblers (8)
5. Conjunction (3)
6. Feline animal (3)
7. Accelerator (8)
8. Silence (4)
9. Post (4)
11. Material from which metal is extracted (3)
13. Opposite of "more" (4)
16. American motorway (7)
18. Attach (6)
21. Making journeys (6)
24. Part of a lorry or plane for the driver or pilot (5)
26. 3rd person singular of "to do" (4)
29. Expression of pleasure or surprise (2)
30. Americans call it a truck (5)
31. Lorries carry it (7)
32. Opposite of "full beam" (6)
35. Before time (5)
37. Move into the right position (6)
38. You put it in the ignition (3)
40. Expressing sudden pain (2)
41. Vehicle with fewer windows for carrying things (3)
42. Ships carry it (5)
43. Farmyard building (4)
46. Some or "_ _ _" (3)

24. TRANSPORT

Crossword answer key

Completed grid (# = shaded square):

```
 1       2        3      4    5        6          7       8
 B  O  O  T  #  J  A  F  F  A  #  C  L  U  T  C  H  H
 E  #  R  U  #  O  #  N  #  A  #  H  #  #  #  #  #  U
 A  M  A  I  N  R  O  A  D  # 10 T  O  U  R  I  S  M  #
9          (11 O)
12 M  E  A  N  #  C  #  T  # 13 L  R  O  #  H  #  #  #  #
 # 14 I  S  T  # 15 P  A  V  E  M  E  N  T  #  #  #  #  #
16 H  E  L  P  I  A  #  S  # 17 T  O 18 F  U  #  #  #  #  #
 I 19 O  N  O  T  # 20 S 21 T  #  #  L  #  A  #  #  #  #  #
22 G  E  A  R  N  # 23 H  I 24 C 25 R  E  V  E  R  S  E  #  #
 H  #  T  # 26 D  #  A  #  A  #  #  #  T  #  E  #  #  #
27 W  A  Y  #  O  #  B  # 28 V 29 E 30 A  L  #  #  E  #  #  #
 A  # 31 F  I  R  E  D  # 32 D  I  E  # 33 H  O  R  N  #  #
34 Y 35 E  A  R  # 36 S  I  G  N 37 A  L  #  R  #  #  #  #  K
 #  A  #  E  #  P  #  #  D  #  #  # 39 R 40 O 41 V  E  #  #
 #  R  I  # 42 C  P  #  #  J  #  #  # 43 B  Y  W  A  Y  #
44 L  U  G  G  A  G  E  #  #  #  #  A  #  #  N  #  #
 #  Y  #  H  R 45 D  O  G  S  #  #  #  R  # 46 A  #  #  #
 #  #  # 47 T  U  G  #  #  # 48 T  U  R  N  I  N  G  G
 #  #  #  #  #  O  #  #  #  #  #  #  #  #  #  Y  #  #
```

25. TRAVEL

25.1 Find the "odd one out".

[There may be more than one answer. Give your reasons.]

1.	A) a charter	B) a schedule	C) a timetable
2.	A) a journey	B) a lift	C) a ride
3.	A) an admission charge	B) an entrance fee	C) a fare
4.	A) destination	B) goal	C) terminus
5.	A) to book	B) to check in	C) to reserve
6.	A) an adventurer	B) an explorer	C) an investigator
7.	A) a desert	B) a dessert	C) a pudding

25.2 Short text (see page 176 for comprehension questions)

Students often manage to travel long distances on very limited **budgets**. The secret is to find cheap travel, food and accommodation.

In the 1960s, British students did this through **hitchhiking** and **youth hostelling**. This can still be done today, though **drivers** are now much more reluctant to offer **lifts** to strangers. **Youth hostels** are also more expensive as they now tend to offer a greater level of comfort. **Hostellers** used to carry their own **sheet sleeping bags** and would expect to sleep in **bunk beds**, often within large **single sex dormitories**. A long walk to one of few outside toilets was not uncommon.

Today, other possibilities present themselves to people living near one of Britain's **international airports**. Hopping on a flight can be done very cheaply. The cost of international **rail travel** is often greater, though it is preferable to pay the extra if you are concerned about your **carbon footprint** and the effects of burning aviation fuel on **global warming**.

Another challenge for those who are trying to economise is finding **reasonably priced accommodation**. This should be arranged well before you arrive at your **holiday destination**, since so much booking is done today on the internet. It is better to be first in the queue rather than last.

25. TRAVEL

25.3   Dialogue - read aloud in pairs

A: *Which is your favourite* country apart from your own?

B: *I suppose I've got a soft spot for* Sweden.

A: *Isn't it rather* cold there?

B: *Well yes, but if* you visit it in June, it's extremely beautiful.

A: *What do you like about it?*

B: *Above all,* the feeling *of* space, the wonderful lakes and the thoughtful city planning. *You have the impression that* people are well looked after, whether they're young or elderly. They have good sports facilities, hospitals and schools. Prices are rather expensive, *but maybe that's a good thing.*

A: *How do you mean?*

B: *I mean that* the country isn't inundated with tourists. It hasn't been ruined by time-share developments or scores of ugly hotels, bars and discos. It's just itself.

A: *Is there anything to do or see?*

B: *Yes, plenty.* Stockholm's among the most attractive capitals in Europe. You can visit an open-air museum and observe several different traditional crafts such as spinning wool, candle-making and glass-blowing. *It's perfect for* short outings, boat trips around the islands and visits to show-piece villages such as Sigtuna.

A: *Where's that?*

B: *It's just a bus ride away from* Stockholm. The high street in Sigtuna is simply charming. It's full of small shops which seem to be from another era. There's a delightful church and the view over the lake is magnificent.

A: *And I gather it isn't* a tourist village?

B: *Well, yes and no.* Sigtuna certainly attracts visitors, *though you'll probably* meet as many Swedes there as foreigners.

A: *Where can I go after* Stockholm?

B: *There are many choices.* You can travel north to see the midnight sun and to visit the polar bears. You can take the night train south west to Copenhagen, the home of Carlsberg beer, or

25. TRAVEL

else head south towards Berlin. You can take the ferry east to Finland, or take the seven hour train journey across the country to Gothenberg passing many spectacular lakes on the way.

25.4   Questions - discuss in pairs or groups

1.   How many countries have you visited and which is your favourite country apart from your own? Explain why?

2.   Would you like to live permanently in another country? Why or why not?

3.   Which is the longest journey you have ever made? How did you travel? What events do you remember on the way?

4.   Which is your favourite journey for beautiful scenery? Describe what there is to see.

5.   Which capital city is your favourite? How do you like to spend your time there?

6.   Do you enjoy touring - travelling from place to place? Describe one of your itineraries?

7.   Do you suffer from travel sickness or anxiety in cars boats or planes? If so, what do you do to overcome these problems?

8.   Do you buy travel insurance before going to visit other countries? What worries would make you take out insurance?

9.   Imagine you are an explorer and have the opportunity to make a big journey. Which continent would you visit? Where would you go? What would you hope to see?

10.   Is organised travel the best way of learning about the world?

Dictionary reference

Hitchhiking: travelling around getting free lifts in passing vehicles owned by people you don't know. You signal for vehicles to stop by displaying your thumb. Popular during the 1960s, but went out of fashion as both drivers and those thumbing lifts began to worry more about their personal safety.

Youth hostelling: travelling around making overnight stays in youth hostels, low-priced accommodation intended originally for young people, but available for some time to all age groups.

147

25. TRAVEL

25.5 Crossword

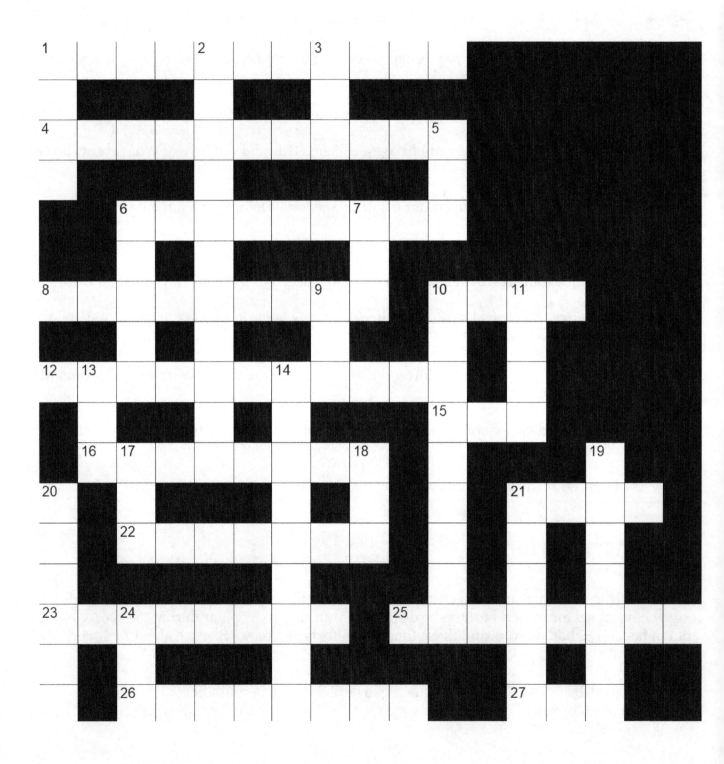

25. TRAVEL

Clues

ACROSS
1. Accommodation for young travellers (5,6)
4. The opposite of "town" (11)
6. Public flight according to a regular timetable (9)
8. Room where people sleep (9)
10. A ride in a car (4)
12. The place where you are going (11)
15. Opposite of "live" (3)
16. Aisles or narrow passages giving access to boats or planes (8)
21. To reserve (4)
22. Special holiday flight (7)
23. Adventurer (8)
25. Bus station - the end of the line (8)
26. View data (8)
27. Old English for "no" (3)

DOWN
1. Young Men's Christian Association (4)
2. Thumbing a lift (11)
3. Help! (3)
5. The final point in a journey (3)
6. Blisters on your feet? (4)
7. Past tense of "lie" (3)
9. Rodent (3)
10. Scenery (9)
11. Money paid for a bus ride (4)
13. Which came first - the chicken or the _ _ _ ? (3)
14. Flat (9)
17. Part of a circle (3)
18. Polite form of address when talking to men (3)
19. Trip (7)
20. The Sahara, for example (6)
21. Person who serves drinks in a pub (6)
24. Domestic animal (3)

25. TRAVEL

Crossword answer key

Across / Down answers:

- 1 YOUTH HOSTEL
- 4 COUNTRYSIDE
- 6 SCHEDULED
- 8 DORMITORY
- 10 LIFT
- 12 DESTINATION
- 15 DIE
- 16 GANGWAYS
- 21 BOOK
- 22 CHARTER
- 23 EXPLORER
- 25 TERMINUS
- 26 TELETEXT
- 27 NAY

26. VIOLENCE

26.1   Find the "odd one out".

[There may be more than one answer. Give your reasons.]

1.   A) an assassin   B) a murderer   C) a killer

2.   A) to hunt   B) to follow   C) to stalk

3.   A) to assault   B) to harass   C) to pester

4.   A) a pacifist   B) a warmonger   C) a conscientious objector

5.   A) a bow and arrow   B) a combat knife   C) a handgun

6.   A) to batter   B) to beat   C) to club

7.   A) to bully   B) to provoke   C) to tease

26.2   Short text (see page 176 for comprehension questions)

There have been several **crimes** which have led British people to reflect on the **causes** of **violence** in our society. One case involved a married couple, who **sexually abused** a number of women, **murdered** them and then **buried** them under their house. A second case involved a member of a **gun club**, who walked into the sports hall of a Primary School and **gunned down** all the members of a class and their teacher. A third case involved two young boys who **battered** a baby boy **to death** after **abducting** him from a shopping centre.

Crimes involving both violence and sexual abuse lead to attempts to limit the availability of **media content** which links the two.

Crimes involving guns have led to legislation in Britain banning the possession of **handguns** in spite of the strong opposition put up by **shooting clubs**. Many parents refuse to buy **toy guns** for their children, not wanting them to associate **war** with **play**. It is difficult to **shelter** children in this way since they are constantly exposed to **violence as entertainment** in the form of **books, comics** and **television cartoons**.

The case involving the young boys led many people to ask whether violence is **inborn** or whether it results from **poor parenting**, failure to **supervise** what children are watching or to set **parental controls**, for example. Current concern is directed towards **the Internet**. The **lack of censorship** means that children can search for **potentially damaging** texts and pictures.

26. VIOLENCE

26.3   Dialogue - read aloud in pairs

A: *What do you think are the causes of* the increase in violence in our society?

B: *Without doubt,* television *has a lot to answer for.*

A: *In what way?*

B: *You've only got to* switch on a film *and you'll see* a violent incident every five or ten minutes on average. *Even* the news bulletins dwell on violence.

A: But on the news, that's violence which actually happens, *isn't it?*

B: *Yes, but* other things happen in the world which aren't violent.

A: *Well, maybe* they don't qualify as news.

B: *In that case, you're saying that* the news isn't representative of what's happening around us.

A: *Well, neither are* Shakespeare's plays. Many of those are centred on wars and tragedies. Novels too are usually based on conflict. That's what gives them their interest value.

B: *The problem with* television *is that* the images of violence are highly graphic and they're shown to us again and again. *Some people are easily influenced by* visual images. Young children may come to believe that the world's like that.

A: *That's highly unlikely.* Everybody understands that films and plays contain drama and that the purpose of the news is to report on what's wrong.

B: *I think you underestimate* the damage that can be done by all this focus on hatred. *You only have to* visit a war zone to see how the minds of young children are twisted by killings, torture and executions.

A: *Come on!* The films we see on TV don't go that far. *At least* there's some censorship.

B: *Now you're saying* that you want good, clean violence on TV. You want it to look clinical. *I'm beginning to think* it would be a good thing if we were shown genocide...if war correspondents showed us what they meant by collateral damage, instead of sanitising violence. Viewers would soon get sick of seeing the real thing.

A: *Make up your mind*! Do you want more or less violence on TV?

B: More of the real world and less sanitised violence.

26. VIOLENCE

26.4   Questions - discuss in pairs or groups

1.   "There should be strict censorship of films and news bulletins on television to prevent children from copying violent incidents." Do you agree?

2.   "Cartoons like "Tom & Jerry" and "Popeye" teach children the wrong lessons." Do you agree?

3.   "Television cameras should not record crowd disturbances during sporting events such as football matches." What do you think?

4.   Is the nuclear deterrent or the threat of extreme violence the best way to keep the peace?

5.   The Peace Pledge Union asks its supporters to renounce war and not to support any kind of war. Do you think this promise is commendable or naive?

6.   "In most countries, military training which prepares people for violence against an enemy, should be replaced by schemes to serve the community." Do you agree?

7.   "Nobody should be permitted to own a handgun for a hobby." What do you think?

8.   "Parents should not buy toy guns or war toys for their children." Do you agree?

9.   How effective do you think are forms of nonviolent direct action as practised by (a) Mahatma Gandhi in opposing British colonialism in India (b) campaigns defending the natural world such as Greenpeace and Extinction Rebellion?

Dictionary reference

A stalker: a person who harasses another person often over a period of time by watching, contacting or following them when their attention is unwanted.

A warmonger: a person who continually promotes war.

Nonviolent direct action: examples range from occupying oil rigs, bridges or trees to boycotts, marches, demonstrations and silent vigils.

Civil disobedience: refusal to obey the demands of a government or occupying power without resorting to violence.

A pledge: a firm promise.

A deterrent: something that discourages people from doing something for fear of the consequences.

26. VIOLENCE

26.5   Crossword

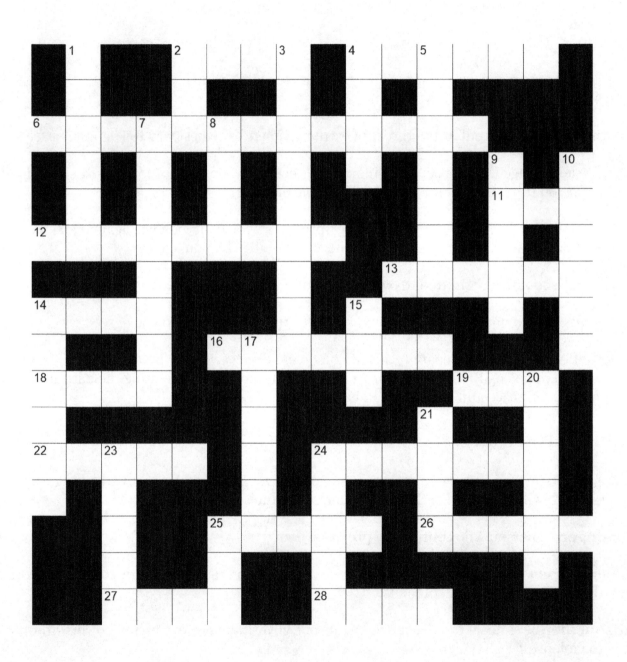

26. VIOLENCE

Clues

ACROSS
2. Become larger in size (4)
4. Sailor who becomes stronger after eating spinach (6)
6. Protest march, for example (13)
11. Inflated feeling of pride (3)
12. Something that discourages others from doing something (9)
13. To edit or suppress news before public release on the grounds of obscenity or security (6)
14. To strike repeatedly (4)
16. A filmed sequence of drawings using animation (7)
18. Rip (4)
19. Residue left when material is burned (3)
22. A mistake (5)
24. A person who follows and pesters another obsessively (7)
25. Wander from the right path (5)
26. A loud explosion (5)
27. Kill (4)
28. Strike with the foot (4)

DOWN
1. A firm promise (6)
2. A firearm (3)
3. A person who constantly promotes war (9)
4. Way or route (4)
5. Incite to anger (7)
7. Protester (8)
8. Create trouble or agitate (4)
9. Make fun of someone playfully or unkindly or annoyingly (5)
10. Ghastly (6)
14. To strike repeatedly with hard blows (6)
15. A lout or hooligan (3)
17. To lead away (6)
20. To pester (6)
21. To strike with heavy stick with thick end (4)
23. Dangers (5)
24. Hit with hand (5)
25. Speak or utter something (3)

26. VIOLENCE

Crossword answer key

27. WORK

27.1   Find the "odd one out".

[There may be more than one answer. Give your reasons.]

1.   A) an application   B) a post   C) a vacancy

2.   A) an applicant   B) a candidate   C) an interviewer

3.   A) an employee   B) an employer   C) a worker

4.   A) an industrial dispute B) a lockout   C) a strike

5.   A) a foreman   B) a shop steward   C) a union representative

6.   A) an apprentice   B) a probationer   C) a trainee

7)   A) a department   B) a division   C) a district

8)   A) wages   B) salary   C) pay

27.2   Short text (see page 177 for comprehension questions)

People in Britain used to look for **jobs** in the **Situations Vacant** column of national or local newspapers, at **Job Centres** and **Employment Agencies**, but the Internet now makes the search much easier. Many companies now post **job openings** directly on their own websites under the "**Careers**" or "Jobs" section. There are also dedicated websites such as **Glassdoor** and **LinkedIn** which offer vast numbers of **job opportunities** and also allow job seekers to have **workplace conversations**.

Before **applying** for a job, you should check that you meet the **requirements**. When you create an account on your chosen website, you are usually prompted to offer profile information including your **educational history**, **qualifications** and **previous work experience**. You can also upload your **curriculum vitae.**

If you **make the right impression,** you will be invited to an **interview**; otherwise you will probably receive an email saying: "we regret to inform you that your application has been unsuccessful." The successful **applicant** should be given a **contract of employment** which will contain the **job description** and the **terms and conditions**. You show your acceptance of these by **signing the contract**.

After you have started your new job, you may be invited to join a **trade union**. If so, you will probably be introduced to your **shop steward**, the trade union **official** who will represent you and

27. WORK

your **colleagues** in negotiations with **management**. Sooner or later, you will meet your **boss**. The person who you **report to**, could also be called a **line manager** or **director.** In factories, **workers** often take their orders from a **team leader** or **foreman**, who acts as an **intermediary** between the **employer** and the **employees**.

27.3 Dialogue - read aloud in pairs

A: *Do people* in Britain work hard?

B: *I'd say they do.* Jobs are so hard to get that if you're lucky enough to have one, you know that you're expected to pull your weight.

A: *What are the conditions* of work *like*?

B: They vary tremendously between jobs. You can see what they're like for people working in supermarket checkouts. They have to keep up or else shoppers or their supervisors get angry.

A: *How about in* schools?

B: Schoolteachers have plenty to do now that they have to administer standardised achievement tests and key stage assessments as part of the National Curriculum. *In many cases,* they've had to stop running clubs and societies after school. They used to do this voluntarily, but now they're tied up with all this paperwork.

A: *Do you think that* public sector workers such as teachers, doctors, nurses and fire fighters should be allowed to strike?

B: *Not if they're* properly rewarded. Their unions should come together with the employers and negotiate no-strike agreements.

A: *What if* the employers decide to introduce new working practices? *After all, things can't remain the same for ever.*

B: Any change in conditions should be negotiated as well.

A: *And what happens if* the two sides can't agree?

B: Then the dispute should go to arbitration. What's needed is an independent body to mediate in industrial disputes. It might sometimes have to impose a settlement.

A: Surely, nobody can force people to go to work, if they really don't want to.

27. WORK

B: *Then* they risk losing their jobs. *It is wrong to* leave hospital patients without doctors and nurses. Likewise, strikes among teachers can severely disrupt the education of our children.

A: *So you don't think everybody should* have the right to strike?

B: *Well, I think everybody should* have the right to join a trade union. This allows free collective bargaining. *You can't have* every worker making separate deals with management. The strike weapon should only be used as a last resort if arbitration fails. Employees should know that management may impose a lockout.

27.4   Questions - discuss in pairs or groups

1.   What ratio of work to leisure would be your ideal? Answer using percentages.

2.   Are the people in your country famous for working hard or for having a good social life?

3.   What jobs would you most and least like to do?

4.   What jobs have you done in your life and what did you like and dislike about them?

5.   Which age-groups are worst affected by unemployment in your country? Should people who have never worked before be entitled to unemployment benefit?

6.   What are the causes of unemployment and how is the problem solved in your country?

7.   Do women in your country have the same job opportunities and pay as men do?

8.   Are there many migrant workers in your country? If so, what kind of jobs do they do? What are their working conditions like?

9.   Do people leave your country to find work in other countries? Where do they go? What sort of jobs do they get? Are they made welcome?

10. Do workers in your country pay a lot of income tax to the government? Do people with large salaries pay a much higher rate of tax than other workers? Do you think they should?

11. Do you think that every worker should have the right to join a Trade Union?

12. Do you think that every worker, (including doctors, nurses, teachers, the police, ambulance crews and fire fighters), should have the right to go on strike?

27. WORK

27.5   Crossword

27. WORK

Clues

ACROSS

2. Conflict between employer and employees (7)
4. The rules (3)
6. Unemployment benefit (4)
8. Trainee (10)
10. White collar pay (6)
11. Skilled (4)
14. Facts (4
15. Union representative (4,7)
17. Worker (8)
18. Idiot (4)
19. Formal written request for employment (11)
23. Your colleagues might buy you one on your birthday (4)
24. Tube-shaped double-reed woodwind instrument with deep tone (4)
25. The boss (8)
28. Confederation of British Industry (3)
29. Toilet (3)
30. Person who asks questions to job applicants (11)
33. Person requesting employment (9)
36. Jobs column in newspaper (10,6)
38. N. America (3)
39. Person being considered for a job (9)
43. Organisation or boss for whom one works (8)
45. Previous work (10)
46. Mass protest in which employees withdraw their labour (6)

DOWN

1. Happenings (6)
2. Part of the company (10)
3. Income (3)
5. Blue collar pay (5)
6. Outline of the job (11)
7. Examination passes (14)
9. What the employee has to do (6)
12. Part of a shirt seen around the neck (6)
13. The employer's needs (12)
14. Two people working together (3)
16. Tactic to prevent strikers from resuming work (7)
20. Ring or call (5)
21. Vacancy (8)
22. Work-mate (9)
26. Agreement between employer and employee (8)
27. Worker taken on for a trial period (11)
28. Worker's hat (3)
31. The ruling collective (10)
32. Target (4)
34. Surprise or shock (4)
35. Job (4)
37. Trade Union (2)
39. Curriculum vitae (2)
40. Confess (5)
41. Obtain money for work (4)
42. Film company (5)
44. To cut jobs for example (3)

27. WORK

Crossword answer key

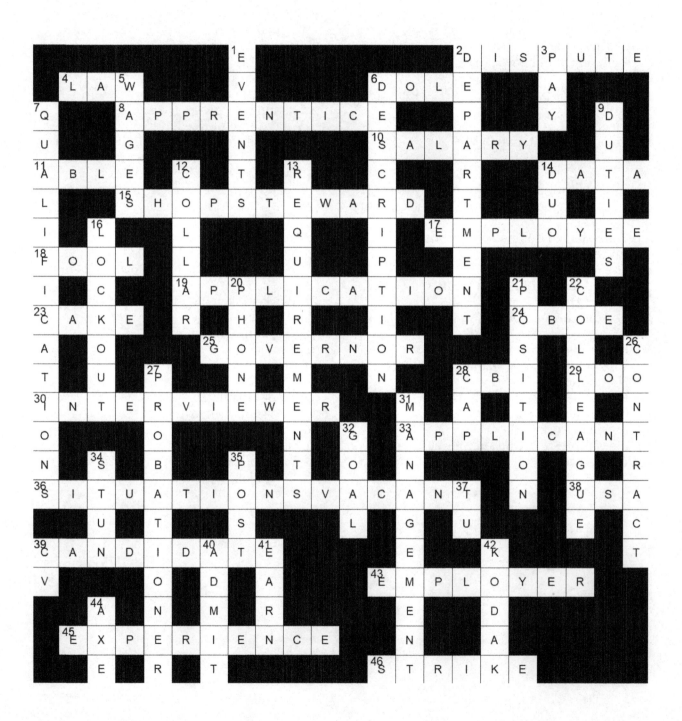

28. YOUTH & OLD AGE

28.1   Find the "odd one out".

[There may be more than one answer. Give your reasons.]

1.	A) experience	B) innocence	C) naivety
2.	A) an adolescent	B) a juvenile	C) a youth
3.	A) a couch potato	B) a tv addict	C) a zombie
4.	A) forgetful	B) confused	C) clumsy
5.	A) an octogenarian	B) a pensioner	C) a senior citizen
6.	A) elderly	B) old	C) antique
7.	A) antiquated	B) old-fashioned	C) veteran
8.	A) to respect	B) to revere	C) to worship

28.2   Short text (see page 177 for comprehension questions)

Youth is associated with **innocence, beauty, good health, energy, idealism, curiosity, immaturity, inexperience** and **rebellion.** Old age often implies **experience, wisdom, fatigue, failing health** and **conservatism.** For some people it is a time of **fulfilment** and **contentment;** for others it may involve **cynicism** and **bitterness.** It is sometimes associated with **senility** when people are **forgetful** or **easily confused.** The physical differences between **the young** and **the elderly** are obvious. The **average age** of competitors in the World Cup or the Olympic Games is likely to be under 35. Medical records show that **pensioners** require more health treatments than other **age groups.**

However, the descriptions of character relate more closely to fiction rather than to actuality. The contrast between the **innocence of youth** and the **experience of adulthood** is established both in William Blake's poetry and William Shakespeare's plays. Shakespeare's young lovers are much too **innocent** and **inexperienced** to engage in vandalism, joyriding or drug trafficking, yet magistrates in Britain today are asking for tougher sentencing powers to combat **juvenile crime.** Many young **teenagers** are now **experienced offenders.**

The notion of youth being **rebellious** could possibly date from the 1960s when there were many **student protests** in Western Europe and the U.S.A. Yet in many other countries, young people are careful to observe **the status quo. Respect for elders** still seems to be more prevalent in Asia and the Middle East than in Western Europe and the U.S.A.

28. YOUTH & OLD AGE

28.3 Dialogue - read aloud in pairs

A: *Do you think that* the young have anything to learn from the elderly *and vice versa?*

B: Well, older people *are said to* have more experience than younger ones.

A: *I've heard that argument time and time again,* but nobody ever says what experience!

B: *I'd've thought that was obvious.* They've lived through personal and family relationships. In many cases, they've bought and sold houses. They've witnessed ups and downs in their careers. They're often experts on matters of health ranging from minor ailments to major operations. Some of them have been round the world.

A: But do these achievements really relate to the problems of young people today?

B: They have to, *somewhere along the line. What I'm saying is that* older people have been there before. They've had the problems and found the solutions. They've plenty to pass on.

A: *I'm not sure that it works like that. You see,* today's young live in a different age. *For a start,* they don't go looking for information on the shelves of their local reference library. If they need any kind of advice, they'll find it on the Internet. *I don't suppose* their grandparents will know what the search commands are.

B: *It seems that you're confusing* the quantity of information you can find on websites with the quality of information you can get from parents and relatives. Nobody knows you better than someone in your own family. *Let's look at the other side of the coin.* What can the young teach the elderly?

A If the elderly are receptive, they could in fact share in some of the benefits of information technology. Think of all the things that are now done online and think of all the useful apps which young people now have on their smartphones. Some of this software is powered by Artificial Intelligence. Applications such as ChatGPT can help with all types of queries and searches for information. They can be really valuable to all age groups.

B: *I wonder whether that's the case. Isn't it rather that* older people enjoy getting out and about and meeting people face to face. *Don't you think they're right to be* suspicious of technology which is turning us all into screen addicts and zombies. The young are so hooked on these electronic toys that they can't really see where they're going. The elderly don't need all this virtual reality. They are content to listen to the trees rustling in the wind, to smell the summer grass and to watch the setting sun.

28. YOUTH & OLD AGE

28.4 Questions - discuss in pairs or groups

1. Are young people generally more selfish than their parents and grandparents?

2. Should adults try to teach young people lessons, such as the dangers of drinking too much, taking drugs or entering into unsuitable relationships, or should they leave them alone to find out about these things for themselves?

3. What do you think is the best age to be? Explain your opinion.

4. Most countries give young people rights as they reach a certain age. For example, British people can legally consent to sex or fight for their country at the age of 16; they can drink, vote and drive a car when they are 18. Does your country have similar laws? Do you think that any of the age limits need changing?

5. Should young people have to do some form of military or community service by law?

6. Should people in their late 60s be obliged to retire from their jobs in order to make way for younger workers?

7. Are there many things that the old can teach the young or are they hopelessly out of touch by the time they reach a certain age?

8. In most countries, compulsory education is targeted at 5 to 16 year olds. Would it be better to offer it to older people who want to learn rather than young people who prefer not to be in school?

9. In Russia, China and many other countries, there is a tradition of choosing leaders who are advanced in years. Do you think that older people make better leaders?

10. Many elderly people have disabilities which limit their mobility. Do buses, shops and public buildings in your country provide easy access for the disabled or are your towns and cities designed mainly for the young and able-bodied?

11. Should the elderly be expected to pay for residential care out of their own savings or should appropriate accommodation and nursing be provided by the taxpayer?

Dictionary reference

Adolescent: generally defined as a person aged between puberty and 18.

Zombie: a dull, apathetic person who does not appear to be thinking about what they are doing.

28. YOUTH & OLD AGE

28.5 Crossword

28. YOUTH & OLD AGE

Clues

ACROSS
1. A person who likes lazing at home, particularly watching TV (5,6)
6. Try to cure (5)
8. A person over 67 years of age (6,7)
10. Small rubber object with two or three metal pins (4)
12. Not in good health - out of practice (5)
13. Out of date or old-fashioned (10)
18. Period of history (3)
19. Not tight (5)
21. A polite word for old (7)
22. Naivety or freedom from moral wrong (9)
23. Young adult (10)
25. Alternative to coffee (3)
26. Not hers (3)
28. Short for "Edward" (3)
33. Young person, not old enough to vote (8)
34. The genuine thing (6)
35. Opposite of "do up" (4)
37. Have a connection with (6)
38. Nativity (5)
39. A dull or apathetic person (6)

DOWN
1. Small American coin (4)
2. Unidentified Flying Object (3)
3. Gain unauthorised access to data in a computer (4)
4. A person in their eighties (12)
5. Possess (3)
7. Not loose (5)
9. Knowledge resulting from practical acquaintance with facts or events (10)
10. A retired person (9)
11. Adult; complete in natural development (6)
14. Made less wild (5)
15. The length of time that a person has existed (3)
16. A person who has grown old in military service or in an occupation (7)
17. Not good at remembering to do things (9)
20. To adore as divine (7)
23. A word usually used to describe old objects of some value (7)
24. Opposite of "young" (3)
27. Opposite of "later" (6)
29. Hold in deep respect (6)
30. Having masculine vigour or strength (6)
31. State of fitness (6)
32. Used for biting (5)
36. A unit of electrical resistance (3)
38. Exist (2)

28. YOUTH & OLD AGE

Crossword answer key

	¹C	O	U	²C	H	³P	O	T	A	T	⁵O		⁶T	R	E	A	⁷T
	E			F		A		C			W						I
⁸S	E	N	I	O	R	C	I	T	I	Z	⁹E	N		¹⁰P	L	U	G
	T			K		O		G			X			E			H
¹¹M						G					P			¹²U	N	F	I	T
¹³A	N	¹⁴T	I	Q	U	¹⁵A	T	E	D		E			S		
T		A		G		N		R			I			I		¹⁶V
U		M	¹⁷F		¹⁸E	R	A		I		¹⁹L	O	O	S	E
R		E	O		R			E		²⁰W	N		T
²¹E	L	D	E	R	L	Y		I		²²I	N	N	O	C	E	N	C	E
		G						A			C			O	R	R	R
²³A	D	²⁴O	L	E	S	C	E	N	T		E	S		²⁵T	E	A
N		L		T							²⁶H	I	²⁷S	N
²⁸T	E	D		F		²⁹R		³⁰V		³¹H	I	O		³²T
I		³³J	U	V	E	N	I	L	E		³⁴P	R	O	P	E	R
Q		L				V		R		A			N		E
³⁵U	N	D	³⁶O			E		I		L			T
E			H		³⁷R	E	L	A	T	E		³⁸B	I	R	T	H
	³⁹Z	O	M	B	I	E		E		H		E

168

COMPREHENSION QUESTIONS

1.2 ALTERNATIVE BELIEFS - Short Text (page 1)

¶1 What is the difference between conventional and alternative beliefs?

¶2 Is the work of mediums and clairvoyants based on mainstream science?

¶3 What powers do mediums claim to possess? What are the meetings called where they exercise these powers?

¶4. What do clairvoyants claim to do? How do cynics explain the successes of clairvoyants?

2.2 ANIMAL WELFARE - Short Text (page 7)

¶1 How are the British said to regard animals?

¶2. What are the expenses associated with keeping animals as domestic pets?

¶3. What evidence do you see in supermarkets of poor regard for animal welfare?

¶4. Why are many people in Britain turning to vegetarian diets?

3.2 THE ARTS - Short Text (page 13)

¶1 What evidence is there to suggest that the arts cover an extremely wide field?

¶2. In what form does literature first present itself to young children?

¶3. Are television soap operas generally more popular than the plays of William Shakespeare?

¶4. Which has the biggest market - opera, ballet or classical music?

4.2 CRIME & PUNISHMENT - Short Text (page 19)

¶1 Do store managers always report shoplifters to the police?

¶2. Why may a store manager not wish to prosecute a shoplifter?

COMPREHENSION QUESTIONS

¶3. What is the task of the twelve members of the jury in a court of law?

¶4. What are the different outcomes if a defendant is found "guilty" or "not guilty"?

5.2 CULTURAL DIFFERENCES - Short Text (page 25)

¶1 What factors have contributed to different waves of immigration?

¶2 Can you name four historical groups who have migrated to Britain and two more recent groups?

¶3. How is successful migration reflected in the food which people eat and in cultural events?

¶4. In what conditions does migration prove less successful?

6.2 ECONOMICS - Short Text (page 31)

¶1 Which are the three main branches of economics?

¶2. How is microeconomic theory usually introduced? What branch of economics deals with monetary and fiscal policies at government level?

¶3. Why do course books in Applied Economics need to be revised frequently? Name some ways that the state can act to control markets through government policy.

¶4. Why is Britain's economic history especially interesting?

7.2 EDUCATION - Short Text (page 37)

¶1 During what age range is education compulsory in the UK? What options do pupils have after they leave secondary school?

¶2 How has further education changed over recent decades?

¶3. Why is the phrase "public school" confusing to people learning about British education?

¶4 What is the difference between "comprehensive" and "grammar" schools? What are the arguments for and against both?

COMPREHENSION QUESTIONS

8.2 ENVIRONMENT - Short Text (page 43)

¶1 Name three organisations which campaign for a cleaner, healthier and less polluted environment.

¶2. Name some of the ways that Greenpeace attempts to embarrass governments and large companies.

¶3. Give examples of some of the local initiatives taken by Friends of The Earth to raise people's awareness of green issues.

¶4 Why has the UK's Green Party been growing in popularity? How has the green movement influenced the agendas of the UK's major political parties? Give an example in terms of a major government policy.

¶5. What has prompted the British public to recognise the need for a greener lifestyle?

9.2 FASHION - Short Text (page 49)

¶1 Give three examples of industries where fashion is especially important.

¶2 What features often accompany changes in design?

¶3. How are fashion models used to sell products?

¶4. Give three examples of how fashion can sometimes cause controversy?

10.2 FOOD - Short Text (page 55)

¶1. What is the difference between "a cook" and "a cooker"?

¶2. Which cooking techniques are associated with (a) hot plates (b) the grill and (c) the oven? What is the difference between "a roast potato" and "a baked potato"?

¶3. Which kitchen implement is usually used to mash a potato? What substance is often added to give a smoother texture?

COMPREHENSION QUESTIONS

11.2 HEALTH - Short Text (page 61)

¶1 What does the NHS stand for? When is it especially useful?

¶2. What is the speciality of an orthopaedic surgeon? What are the medical terms used to describe your "thigh bone" and your "kneecap"?

¶3. What is the role of a physiotherapist after a patient has been operated on for a broken leg? Give examples of how a physiotherapist can help at different stages of recovery.

12.2 HOLIDAYS - Short Text (page 67)

¶1 How has the Internet affected the holiday industry over the past 25 years?

¶2. What is an air bed and breakfast? List some of the other things that can be booked online.

¶3. When describing the kind of holiday you want, list some of the important variables.

¶4. How can budgeting and ethical considerations influence your choice of holiday options?

¶5. Give examples of how an Artificial Intelligence system such as ChatGPT can help you plan a holiday?

13.2 LANGUAGE LEARNING - Short Text (page 73)

¶1 In what ways do some language teachers respect the learner as an individual?

¶2. What arguments support the role of the teacher as opposed to non-interference?

¶3. What problems arise when the teaching of modern languages is modelled on the teaching of Latin?

¶4.What are the advantages and disadvantages of the audio-lingual method?

14.2 MALE & FEMALE ROLES - Short Text (page 79)

¶1 Give examples of the growing representation of women in the House of Commons and in the UK's small businesses.

COMPREHENSION QUESTIONS

¶2 In which industry are men still generally favoured for the top jobs?

¶3. What rights did women have to campaign for during the 20th century? What events permitted women to prove their capabilities? Give examples of how women's rights campaigns have focused on language and thought.

¶4. How have men reacted to women's campaigns for equal rights?

15.2 MARRIAGE - Short Text (page 85)

¶1 What evidence is there that the divorce rate in Britain is high?

¶2 What proportion of British babies are born outside of marriage? Does this matter?

¶3 How tolerant are people in Britain of different kinds of relationships? What is the Church of England's attitude towards remarrying people who have already been divorced?

16.2 THE MEDIA - Short Text (page 91)

¶1 What is included when we refer to "the media"?

¶2. How important is it for political parties seeking election to have the support of national newspapers? Why is this slightly less important than it was in the past?

¶3. Are media platforms truly independent, protecting the interests of all people equally?
y
¶4. Describe the system of grades used by media providers and advertising agencies to classify members of the public.

17.2 POLITICAL SYSTEMS - Short Text (page 97)

¶1 What are the three names of Britain's main political party? What are their nicknames?

¶2.What is the difference between the House of Commons and the House of Lords? How much power has the House of Lords?

COMPREHENSION QUESTIONS

¶3. What is the maximum period of government before ruling powers have to call a general election? Do they keep to this timescale? How many parliamentary constituencies does a party have to win to have an overall majority? Describe the jobs of the key posts in the government.

18.2 RELIGION - Short Text (page 103)

¶1 What is the difference between an atheist and an agnostic? What is a humanist and what may humanists have in common with people of religious faiths?

¶2. What is the difference between Protestants and Catholics? Name at least three different ranks within the Church of England. Who is the head of the Church of England?

19.2 RICH WORLD : POOR WORLD - Short Text (page 109)

¶1 What phrases are used to describe the world's rich and poor countries?

¶2 What is meant by the "North South divide" when applied to the world?

¶3.Do most people take the view that charity should begin at home?

¶4. Does the obligation of the rich world to help the poor world relate solely to historical exploitation?

20.2 SCIENCE & TECHNOLOGY - Short Text (page 115)

¶1 Why do many British parents find it difficult to help their children with science and technology homework?

¶2. What research skills are now associated with science and technology? Why is familiarity with computers now essential?

¶3. How was technology as a school subject regarded 30 years ago? How is it regarded as a school subject today? Why has computer literacy continued to become of increasing importance?

COMPREHENSION QUESTIONS

21.2 SOCIETY - Short Text (page 121)

¶1 What were the social trends associated with Britain in the 1940s and 50s?

¶2 How did young people challenge the conventional view of society during the 1960s?

¶3. In what ways is today's society more tolerant than before? What has happened to trust and people's working habits?

22.2 SPORT - Short Text (page 127)

¶1 Name four altitude sports. What kind of people should avoid these sports?

¶2. Name four track and field events. How far is a circuit of a standard track?

¶3. Name six combat games.

¶4 Name nine games played on rectangular courts.

¶5. Name five equestrian sports? Why does horse racing hold an extra attraction to those not taking part?

¶6. Why do field sports require a large area of green? Give five examples.

¶7. Give four examples of floor exercises in gymnastics and four examples of fixed apparatus sports.

¶8. Place the following sports within general categories: (a) shooting (b) swimming (c) cycling (d) skiing.

23.2 TRADITIONS - Short Text (page 133)

¶1 What is it about traditions that many of us welcome? What connections define traditions?

¶2 Name two places in Britain that are associated with legendary people ?

¶3. What objects are associated with annual religious ceremonies? Name three non-religious traditions in the UK annual calendar.

¶4. What are the traditional elements of a British church wedding?

COMPREHENSION QUESTIONS

24.2 TRANSPORT - Short Text (page 139)

¶2. What adjustments should you make when you first get into the driving seat of a car?

¶3. Once the car engine is started which pedals do you depress and which gears do you change into before moving on?

¶4. What is the procedure if you wish to turn right or left?

¶5 . Which controls are usually mounted on the dashboard? Where is the horn situated?

25.2 TRAVEL - Short Text (page 145)

¶1 How do students make a limited budget go a long way?

¶2. How did many students travel cheaply during the 1960s? Describe the sleeping arrangements.

¶3. Why might today's travellers prefer to travel by train rather than take a cheap flight?

¶4. What measures should travellers take if they wish to find reasonably priced accommodation?

26.2 VIOLENCE - Short Text (page 151)

¶1 Describe three crimes which made British people reflect on the causes of violence in their society?

¶2. What action has been taken in an attempt to limit crimes involving violence and sexual abuse?

¶3. What has been done in attempts to limit crimes involving guns? Why is it difficult to shelter children from scenes involving guns?

¶4. What question did many people ask following the case involving two young boys who violently killed a baby? Why are there concerns about the Internet?

COMPREHENSION QUESTIONS

27.2 WORK - Short Text (page 157)

¶1 In the years before the Internet became popular, how did most people look for jobs?

¶2. What should you check before applying for a job? What profile information will good job websites usually demand and what will they allow you to upload in addition?

¶3. What should a contract of employment contain?

¶4.What may you be invited to join after starting a new job? Who may you be introduced to before meeting your boss?

28.2 YOUTH & OLD AGE - Short Text (page 163)

¶1 List nine of the qualities associated with youth and five of the qualities associated with old age.

¶2 Why is it misleading to talk about the "innocence" and "inexperience" of youth?

¶3. How does respect for elders vary in different parts of the world?

COMPREHENSION QUESTIONS

LIST OF 28 TOPICS

01. Alternative Beliefs
02. Animal Welfare
03. The Arts
04. Crime & Punishment
05. Cultural Differences
06. Economics
07. Education
08. Environment
09. Fashion
10. Food
11. Health
12. Holidays
13. Language Learning
14. Male & Female Roles
15. Marriage
16. The Media
17. Political Systems
18. Religion
19. Rich World : Poor World
20. Science & Technology
21. Society
22. Sport
23   Traditions
24. Transport
25   Travel
26. Violence
27   Work
28. Youth & Old Age

EXTRACTS FROM THE DIALOGUES
containing the colloquial formulae used in discussion

1.   ASKING SOMEONE FOR THEIR OPINION ABOUT A TOPIC

Look at the list of 28 topics. Listen to the questions in this section read by your teacher or pair work partner. Each question is repeated twice. As you listen, write down the name of the discussion topic the speaker is asking about.

Ask the opinion of your teacher or pair work partner on a subject of your choice using at least one expression from each of sections 1.1, 1.2, 1.3 and 1.4.

1.1   Yes/No Questions

01   *Do you believe in* horoscopes?

18   *Do you believe in* a God who rewards good and punishes wrongdoing?

04   *Do you think we should* be tougher on crime?

23   *Do you think we should* maintain our traditions or make way for change?

16   *Do you think the Government should* act to curb the power of media barons.... ?

20   *Do you think* that it is possible to get computers to think, learn and act like humans?

27   *Do you think that* public sector workers such as teachers, doctors, nurses and fire fighters should be allowed to strike?

28   *Do you think that* the young have anything to learn from the elderly and vice versa?

07   *Would you consider* sending your child to a grammar school?

11   *Would you ever consider* taking out private health insurance?

1.2   OR Questions

06   *Are you for or against* self-sufficiency?

07   *Would you prefer* your child to be educated privately or by the state?

07   *Would you rather* go to a mixed or single-sex school?

13   *Which should be* the official world language - English or Esperanto?

1.3   WH Questions

02   *What do you think of* fox hunting?

10   *What do you think of* British food?

12   *What do you think of* package holidays?

05   *What do you think is* the problem between the English and the Americans?

26   *What do you think are* the causes of the increase in violence in our society?

15   *What are the advantages and disadvantages of* getting married?

1.4   Negative Yes/No Questions

07   How about boarding schools? *Don't they* teach children how to live together?

15   What are the advantages and disadvantages of getting married? *Don't you think it's better to stay single?*

2.   DELAYING STRATEGIES

Listen to the replies in this section and repeat them exactly as you hear them. You will hear them twice. Working in pairs, create short conversations in which you are asked a difficult question and use a delaying strategy in reply.

08   I can answer that directly.

21   I'll need time to think about that.

05   That's a very interesting question, because (20)

10   That's a difficult question to answer, because

07   To be honest, that's a difficult question, because

11.   That's a very good question. The reality is that

16   What do you mean by that?

04   Well, it depends on what you mean.

15   Well, if you ask me, it all depends on your circumstances.

04   Well... (12 16 20 23 24)

3.   PRESENTING A NUMBER OF ARGUMENTS

Listen to the extracts. As you listen to each one, write down the name of the discussion topic. Working in pairs, create conversations in which you use some of the methods for presenting a number of arguments.

24   *First of all*, Britain is unique in its transport history.

04   *Firstly*, what do you do about miscarriages of justice?

18   *Well, firstly* I'm an agnostic - I don't know whether or not God exists....

19   *Well, firstly* we need to take an interest in developing countries instead of just competing with rich countries.

14   *To begin with*, most women and men want the right to work.

08   *I'd start by* rationing petrol to cut out unnecessary car journeys.

07   *For a start*, it would have to be a mixed school and not a boarding establishment.

09   *There 're two points here. Firstly*, the cost to the environment. Think of all the rain forests. *Secondly*, the advertiser may pay, but the costs are passed on to the consumer.

12   *There are two problems here.* Some of these homes are a long way from bus routes. *Moreover*, bus services can disappear altogether when the tourist season comes to an end.

13   The economic strength of Japan hasn't led to much teaching of Japanese. *You also have to consider* the vast size of the knowledge base available to English speakers - academic research, scientific reports and an infinite number of books and periodicals.

22   *Also*, the very act of hosting the World Cup or the Olympics gives a great boost to tourism.

07   *Again*, that depends on the alternatives. I prefer the comprehensive system, but I wouldn't want my child to be in mixed ability classes for all subjects.

4. GIVING YOUR OPINION ABOUT A TOPIC

4.1   Expressing a strong opinion

Listen to each extract and write down just the phrase used to express an opinion. Each extract is repeated twice.

Working in pairs, create conversations using some of the phrases used for expressing opinions.

09   *In my opinion*, fashion is a complete waste of time, money and resources.

13   *In my opinion*, there's only one choice - English!

03   *In my view*, government money shouldn't be used to support the Arts.

04   *In my reckoning*, if we could lock up juvenile criminals, they'd learn that they couldn't get away with it.

19   *I strongly believe in* preventing problems before they happen. In much the same way as the Japanese prepare for earthquakes, countries with dry climates could have water catchment systems and reservoirs to defend against water shortage.

06   *I definitely think that* countries should be self-sufficient in food and basic necessities.

15   Don't you think it's better to stay single? *Well, if you ask me*, it all depends on your circumstances.

27   *Well, I think* everybody should have the right to join a trade union.

4.2   Expressing a strong value (It's / They're + value adjective)

Listen to each extract and write down just the phrases used to express a strong value or feeling. Each extract is repeated twice.

Write your own mini conversations expressing values or feelings.

07   *It's a nonsense to* keep everybody at the same level regardless of their progress.

17   Their pay is rarely much more than the minimum wage. *It's a scandal,* because many pizza parlours, pubs and burger bars are really being subsidised by the Government.

25   *It's perfect for* short-outings, boat trips around the islands and visits to show-piece villages such as Sigtuna.

27   *It's wrong to* leave hospital patients without doctors and nurses. Likewise, strikes among teachers can severely disrupt the education of our children.

24   *They're ideal for* people who really want to relax and live life at a slower pace.

4.3   Expressing certainty

Listen to each extract and write down just the words used to express certainty or which add authority. Role play your own conversations containing some of the expressions.

11   *According to government statistics*, waiting lists are coming down.

13   *Actually,* Esperanto is closer to European languages than any others.

10   *In fact,* we have some of the top chefs in the world, but only people with a lot of money experience British cooking at its best.

07   *Clearly,* a coeducational environment promotes understanding between boys and girls. It's far more natural.

05   So in what ways are they superior? *Well, obviously* in size. Everything's bigger.

09   *People have always* liked dressing up.

16   *People just won't* continue to accept editorial lines which don't match up with their experience.

26   *Without doubt,* television has a lot to answer for.

16   *There's no doubt that* these large monopolies have a great deal of power. *On the other hand,* Britain is fortunate to have public corporations such as the BBC which get their income from the licence payer rather than advertisers.

19   *Well, there's no doubt that* a proper understanding of their problems is needed before we can go much further. Surely, there are immediate things like food aid to countries hit by drought or famine

12   *Surely,* most of these resorts would have bus services.

15   *Surely,* there's more to marriage than having children.

4.4   Expressing high or low probability

Listen to each extract and write down just the words used to show high or low probability.
Create your own examples using some of the expressions.

06   *I expect that* Japan could adapt. It has a highly skilled workforce and a good technological base.

24   *I believe* you've been working on a transport policy for Britain.

04   *I doubt whether* they could act as an effective deterrent while the detection rate is so low.

13   *I doubt that* many other languages can match the size of the English dictionary.

16   *I doubt that* this would ever happen. The BBC prides itself on its independence...

07   *I'd've thought they'd* be very useful for children without brothers and sisters.

28   *I'd've thought that* was obvious. They've lived through personal and family relationships. They're often experts on matters of health ranging from minor ailments to major operations.

21   *There now seems to be a general acceptance that* Britain is a multi-racial society.

4.5   Expressing fair probability

Listen to each extract and write down just the words used to express assumptions and guesses. Create your own examples showing fair probability.

15   *I guess that* many single people have different priorities or else they believe that they'd make unsuitable parents.

01   *I suppose it's* all part of your total environment. Scientists don't understand everything, but they often observe links between certain phenomena.

28   *I don't suppose* their grandparents will know what the search commands are.

10   *I think it's probably possible to* generalise about what is eaten at main mealtimes.

17   *There's probably a good argument for* raising benefits.

05   *They 're probably* warmer and more friendly, but they're very loud and extrovert to go with it.

26   *I'm beginning to think it would be a good thing if* we were shown genocide... if war correspondents showed us what they meant by collateral damage ...

5.   AGREEING

5.1   Expressing complete agreement

Listen to the extracts. Identify the words used to show full agreement. Do you know any similar expressions? Write two lines of dialogue where these expressions are used.

05   We say one thing and mean another? *Exactly.*

16   You mean, you can't fool all the people all of the time? *Exactly.*

21   You mean it's possible to ignore the Green Party, but you can't ignore their policies when a general consensus of people come to support them? *Exactly.*

17   Once the level of benefit is higher than their take-home pay, why should they do a job? *Precisely*, but the answer isn't to remove benefits from those who really need them.

5.2   Expressing conditional agreement

Listen to the extracts containing words expressing conditional agreement. Write your own example.

18   *I'd agree with you if* the purpose of hell was to rehabilitate people back into heaven, but hell is usually associated with torture and damnation.

22   *I'd certainly agree if* you 're thinking of the World Cup.

6.   DISAGREEING

6.1   Expressing complete disagreement

Listen to the extracts and repeat the words used to show strong disagreement. Create your own dialogue where expressions of strong disagreement are used or respond to opinions voiced by your teacher.

09   In my opinion, fashion is a complete waste of time, money and resources. *I disagree entirely.* The world would be a boring place without change.

03   In my view, government money shouldn't be used to support the Arts. *I'm afraid I can't agree.* Public support for the Arts is the hallmark of a civilised society.

15   It's impossible to generalise about why people prefer married to single status. *Rubbish!* It must be possible to compare living together with someone to living on your own. What about the question of independence?

6.2   Using irony to express disagreement

Listen to the extracts and repeat the exclamations and questions used for ironic effect. Each extract is repeated twice. Write a short exchange including the use of one of these ironic expressions. Do you know any more?

06   Besides, the production lines are often highly mechanised. *Come off it!* Agriculture in developing countries is still fairly labour intensive.

26   *Come on!* The films we see on TV don't go that far. At least there's some censorship.

02   Besides, it's such a cruel way to kill them. *Do you really think so?* Once the first dog had caught up with the fox, death is fairly instant.

6.3   Dismissing an argument as irrelevant or improbable.

Listen to the extracts and repeat the phrases used to dismiss or reject arguments. Each extract is repeated twice.

02   But fox hunting is part of country life. It's one of our traditions
      That's beside the point! Dogfighting and cockfighting were traditions and so was slavery.

23   I bet you can get traditional Spanish wines and beers! *That isn't the point.* I'm talking about soft drinks.

03   *That's highly debatable.* Some of the exhibits you see from contemporary artists are no more than tins of baked beans and piles of bricks.

26   *That's highly unlikely.* Everybody understands that films and plays contain drama and that the purpose of the news is to report on what's wrong.

6.4   Disagreeing diplomatically (through doubt)

Listen to the extracts and repeat the phrases used to cast doubt on arguments. Each extract is repeated twice.

28   The elderly are often confused by modem telephones and automatic switchboards.
      I wonder whether that's the case. Isn't it rather that they enjoy getting out and about instead of sitting next to a telephone?

28   What I'm saying is that older people have been there before. They've had the problems and found the solutions. *I'm not sure that it works like that.* You see today's young live in a different age.

23   If the songs are any good, then surely they'll survive.
      I'm not so sure about that.
      Why not?
      Because traditions are now under attack from mass production and mass marketing.

13   *Well, I'm not sure whether* you can really separate language from culture

6.5   Disagreeing in part (appeal to logic)

Listen to the extracts and identify the phrases used to question the logic or truth of an argument. Each extract is repeated twice.

24 But surely, the canal system is much too slow for industry today.
Not necessarily.

24 By the time you've loaded the goods onto a truck, you might as well do the whole journey by road.
That doesn't necessarily follow. A lot of trade is with Europe and before the Channel Tunnel there was a good container industry.

09 the advertiser may pay, but the costs are passed onto the consumer.
That isn't strictly true. If a company can sell in bulk, prices can be brought down.

7.   COUNTERING

Look at the list of 28 topics. Listen to the extracts in this section and repeat after the speaker. As you repeat, identify the topic which is being discussed.

7.1   Countering directly   (through antithesis)

02 *But* fox hunting is part of country life. It's one of our traditions.

08 *But* public transport is expensive and inconvenient.

13 *But* English has borrowed from the Romans, the Vikings, the Saxons and the French

24 *But* freight trains can't deliver goods from door to door

18 *But* who can say that we will develop into civilised beings? Surely, God has the right to cut his losses!

22 *But* why play the gold medalists' national anthems and why wear stars and stripes on your swimming costumes?

02 *But* if you worked on a farm and your chickens were killed by foxes, you'd think differently.

04 *But* if you detect more crimes, you'll still need prisons.

18 *But* if you followed that line to its logical conclusion, you'd pardon all criminals.

12 *But surely*, you can see what you're getting in the holiday brochure.

17 *But surely*, if you raise benefits too high, people wouldn't bother to work.

24   *But surely*, the canal system is much too slow for industry today.

7.2   Countering politely (through agreement followed by antithesis)

25   *Well yes, but* if you visit it in June, it's extremely beautiful.

01   *Yes, but* a serious astrologer would want to know a person's exact date of birth, not just their star sign.

04   *Yes, but* remember that prisons are often schools for criminals.

05   *Yes, but* we measure our superiority in different ways. Ours is cultural and historical. We believe we're more civilised.

14   *Yes, but it isn't that* women don't want to work. For a start, they suffer more discrimination in the work-place.

26   Yes, *but* other things happen in the world which aren't violent.

7.3   Countering politely (through partial agreement followed by antithesis)

09   *That may be so, but* traditional costumes were made to be worn more than once.

13   *That may be true, but then* you're inviting political conflict. Who is going to decide whether North American culture is superior to Chinese culture?

15   *That may be so, but for most people* the whole point of marriage is to live together and raise a
f   family.

22   *That might have been the case once, but* you forget that mega-stars like Pele and Ali were the products, they could pull crowds and make vast sums of money.

07   *Well, maybe they do, but* they've got to learn to live together. I'm against all forms of segregation.

22   *You may be right* about sport and politics, *but* it can work both ways

7.4   Countering using "well" both to cast doubt and for antithesis

03   Think of all the money that's spent in the souvenir shops of these galleries and museums. *Well* you might as well argue that the government should subsidise all shops.

11   But under the patients' charter, hospitals are meant to treat you within a certain time.
         Well, you know how they get round that one. They make you wait for months before they put
         you on the waiting list.

18   Nobody has to suffer. Everybody is free to choose between right and wrong.
         Well, that depends on whether we really have free will.

7.5   Countering using "after all" "at least" "even so" both for concession and antithesis

23   Why shouldn't they? If they're any good, then surely they'll survive.
         After all, these songs have been handed down for generations.

27   What if the employers decide to introduce new working practices? *After all*, things can't
         remain the same for ever.

26   The films we see on TV don't go that far. *At least* there's some censorship.

13   *But at least* it's culture-free. With Esperanto as the world language, no country would be
         accused of exporting both its language and its culture.

01   *Well, even so*, why should the exact positions of the Sun, Moon and other planets on your date
         of birth have any connection whatsoever with your personality and the future course of your
         life?

06   *Even so,* not all developing countries are food producers. The hamburger farms of those that
         are, make very wasteful use of the land and the profits go mainly to foreign investors.

7.6   Countering using the Negative Yes/No Question

14   Then some people will be out of a job - they could be either women or men.
         Aren't they more often women?

28   The elderly are often confused by modem telephones and automatic switchboards.
         I wonder whether that's the case. Isn't it rather that they enjoy getting out and about instead
         of sitting next to a telephone? *Don't you think* they 're right to be suspicious of technology
         which is turning us all into screen addicts and zombies?

16   Well, it may not be owned, but it is controlled by a Board of Governors appointed by the Prime
         Minister. *Don't you think there's a danger of* self-censorship?

08   Drivers who want more than their rations would have to pay a much higher rate for the extra. The profit could be used to develop environmentally clean vehicles and fast efficient railway networks.
        Don't you think you're being unfair to the private motorist and what about the car industry?

07   Clearly, a coeducational environment promotes understanding between boys and girls. It's far more natural.
        Don't you think they distract one another when they become teenagers?

21   *Don't you think* the vision of the three major parties is more or less the same?

8.   LOGICAL ARGUMENT

Look at the list of 28 topics. Listen to the extracts in this section and repeat after the speaker. As you repeat, write down the name of the topic which is being discussed. Each extract is repeated twice.

8.1   Questions or conclusions based on conditions with "if".

02   *If* farmers really need to kill foxes, *why don't they* just shoot them?

14   *What if* there isn't enough work to go round?

27   *What if* the employers decide to introduce new working practices?

27   *And what happens if* the two sides can't agree?

17   *What would happen then if* state benefits were cut completely?

03   *If* this also makes Britain more attractive for overseas visitors, *so well and good*.

04   *You'd only* use capital punishment *if you were absolutely sure that* you'd convicted the right person.

23   *It'd be O.K. if* they recognised the quality of the songs their grandmother had taught them and went on to sing them to their own grandchildren.

8.2   Questions based on conditions with sentence adverbials " then" and "so"

18   We punish murderers and rapists on Earth, *so why shouldn't* the same people rot in hell?

12   but if you want to go to a nicer locality, you can spend all day getting there.
        Then how do you go about making your own arrangements?

18   Other people are part of the environment and they have a right to react to wrong-doing to protect society. *Then why shouldn't* God send evil people to hell?

06   That's why I'm advocating self-sufficiency as a goal.
      Then can you tell me what's wrong with helping one another out?

8.3   Deduced questions and conclusions with sentence adverbials "In that case" and "so"

01   Scientists... often observe links between certain phenomena.
       In that case, would you describe astrology as a Science?

15   ... the whole point of marriage is to live together and possibly raise a family.
      In that case, it's obvious that children are a commitment for life.

26   Yes, but other things happen in the world which aren't violent.
      Well, maybe they don't qualify as news.
      In that case, you're saying that news isn't representative of what's happening around us.

05   They're probably warmer and more friendly, but they're often very loud and extrovert to go with it.
      So you prefer the British character?

27   Likewise, strikes among teachers can severely disrupt the education of our children.
      So you don't think everybody should have the right to strike?

8.4   Strongly argued questions with "Why"

07   *Why have we got to* create large institutional families? If people decide to have children, then they should value family life.

03   *Why should other people* pay for the exhibition of junk which nobody wants?

11   But you're already paying for the NHS through national insurance.
      Why should you have to insure yourself twice?

17   Once the level of the benefit is higher than their take-home pay, *why should they* do a job?

08   *Why shouldn't those who cause* air and noise pollution do something to reduce it?

06   If mountainous countries like Japan can export good cars, *why shouldn't they* import their food?

9. CLARIFICATION

The teacher or your pair work partner reads the extract. Identify the expression used to ask for clarification and the name of the discussion topic.

9.1 Clarification through short Yes/No Questions inviting illustration or example.

05 They (North Americans) enjoy telling us that they're the best.
And are they right?
Yes, if you measure success purely in dollars ....

11 but the (health) service is under too much pressure to give adequate support.
Can you be a bit more specific?
Certainly. There're thousands of people who are in great pain. Some are waiting for minor surgery while others are waiting for treatment at pain control clinics.

14 but it's possible to give the job to a man with fewer qualifications.
Does that happen?
Perhaps not as much as it used to, but if a woman leaves a job to start a family, it may be very difficult for her to return to full-time work.

9.2 Clarification through "What" or "How" Questions inviting illustration or example.

03 *What's wrong with* creating a few more jobs in the tourist industry? Think of all the money that's spent in the souvenir shops of these galleries and museums.

07 *What's wrong with* mixed ability teaching?
The reality is that people learn subjects such as languages and mathematics at different speeds.

15 *What do you mean?*
I mean that people's situations can be very different. Let's take the very extreme situation of a young woman who marries an old man as an example.

08 *What do you mean by* unnecessary?
Let me explain. Every morning, people go up and down motorways or cross from one side of town to the other in their cars, when they could quite easily take trains or buses

25 Prices are rather expensive, but maybe that's a good thing.
How do you mean?
I mean that the country isn't inundated with tourists. It hasn't been ruined by timeshare developments or scores of ugly hotels, bars and discos.

20   Artificial intelligence systems are improving all the time.
How do you mean?

17   Many pizza parlours, pubs and burger bars are really being subsidised by the Government.
How come?
Because nobody would be able to accept jobs in these places if they didn't have their incomes topped up by the state.

26   Without doubt, television has a lot to answer for.
In what way?
You've only got to switch on a film and you'll see a violent incident every five or ten minutes on average.

9.3   Clarification through "Why" / "Why not" Questions inviting reason, illustration or example.

23   The young are often embarrassed by them (traditions). This is a shame.
Why do you say that?
Let me explain. Take a traditional Japanese song, for example.

24   First of all, Britain is unique in its transport history.
Why's that?
Because of all the transport systems that have been developed in the last 300 years.

22   Not at national or international level.
Why not?
Well, we can hardly keep politics out of the Eurovision song contest. How are we meant to keep it out of football, which has a far greater following?

23   I'm not so sure about that.
Why not?
Because traditions are now under attack from mass production and mass marketing.

9.4   Clarification / Reiteration through reference to subject

Look at the list of 28 topics. Listen to the extracts and write down the name or number of the topic which is being discussed. Each extract is repeated twice.

05   They are usually on the same side in war-time, yet they rarely speak well of one another on a personal level.
Are we talking about a struggle for superiority?

03   *I'm talking about* national institutions, centres of culture which represent the best of Britain's historical and artistic treasures.

23   That isn't the point. *I'm talking about* soft drinks, and few Spanish bars will serve you with "horchata", their own traditional soft drink.

16   *Are you saying that* foreign-based multi-nationals decide who is going to be British Prime Minister.

03   Well you might as well argue that the government should subsidise all shops. *I'm saying that* it's the British tax-payer who pays the bill.

06   *What I'm saying is* that we are too interdependent. Perhaps our populations are too big. That's why I'm advocating self-sufficiency as a goal.

28   *What I'm saying is* that older people have been there before. They've had the problems and found the solutions.

15   *What are you trying to say?* To come to the point, there are so many different motives for marriage that it's impossible to generalise about why people prefer married to single status.

15   That may be so, but for most people the whole point of marriage is to live together and possibly to raise a family. *That's what this discussion's about.*

03   *To come back to the main point*, this isn't only about contemporary, experimental art. I'm talking about the appreciation of great masterpieces which have been acknowledged for centuries.

10.   EXPRESSING SOLUTIONS and ALTERNATIVES

Look at the list of 28 topics. Listen to the extracts in this section and repeat after the speaker. As you repeat, write down the name of the topic which is being discussed. Each extract is repeated twice.

17   *The solution is to* compel all employers to pay a minimum wage. Then you will increase the incentive to work...

04   *The best way to* prevent crime is to convince the people who commit it that they are going to be caught. To remove crime from society, you really have to tackle its causes.

25   *There are many choices. You can* travel north to see the midnight sun... *You can* take the night train to Copenhagen... *You can* take the ferry east to Finland or take the seven hour train journey across the country to Gothenburg.

15   As for the young woman, she may have a lot in common with the old man; *alternatively*, she may be interested in his money.

23   Well, when they reach the age of fifteen, they reject the songs of their childhood. *Instead*, they are into pop or rock songs which will be forgotten within weeks.

06   You see, *the alternative is* to buy food on the world market. We all know that when demand rises, so does the price.

Printed in Dunstable, United Kingdom